Profiles of Best Practices in Academic Library Interlibrary Loan

Edited and with an Introduction and Summary of Key Findings

By Paul Kelsey

©2009   Primary Research Group Inc.

ISBN # 1-57440-122-X

TABLE OF CONTENTS

Participating Institutions

     I. University of Texas at Arlington
    II. Tulane University
   III. University of Minnesota
   IV. Indiana University-Purdue University Indianapolis
    V. Brigham Young University
   VI. University of Tennessee
  VII. Colorado State University
VIII. Oberlin College
   IX. Stony Brook University

About the Editor

Paul Kelsey is currently an independent scholar and editor. He earned an MLIS from the University of Texas at Austin, and an undergraduate degree in Religion from the Colorado College. He has over a decade of experience working in both academic and public libraries. Kelsey has worked both as a collection development coordinator and ILB supervisor at an ARL library and as a circulation librarian at a liberal arts college. The editor has served on several ALA committees and also served for a number of years as a member of USAIN (United States Agricultural Information Network). He is a co-founder of the Louisiana Young Readers' Choice Award and currently resides in Baton Rouge with his family.

Paul's list of selected publications include "The Financial Counseling and Planning Indexing Project: Establishing a Correlation Between Indexing, Total Citations, and Library Holdings", in *Financial Counseling and Planning*, v. 18, no. 1 (2007); Paul Kelsey and Mohan Ramaswamy, "Designing a Successful Library School Field Experience", in *Library Management*, v. 26, no. 6/7 (2005); Paul Kelsey and Sigrid Kelsey, eds., *Outreach Services in Academic and Special Libraries*, Binghamton, NY: The Haworth Press, 2003; and Paul Kelsey and Tom Diamond, "Establishing a Core List of Journals for Forestry: A Citation Analysis from Faculty at Southern Universities" in *College and Research Libraries*, v. 64 (2003).

Introduction

Advances in resource sharing have allowed academic interlibrary loan departments to achieve unprecedented levels of service for their constituents. Participation in multiple resource sharing consortia has emerged as a standard "best practice" for university and college libraries, improving fill rates and turn-around time for article delivery. Academic libraries now almost universally use OCLC's ILLiad as their resource sharing client and deliver articles electronically to constituents via Odyssey. Many academic interlibrary loan departments have implemented local document delivery services "as a best practice," scanning print articles from their collections and delivering them electronically to patrons. Libraries continue to negotiate lending rights aggressively in licensing provisions for electronic journal subscriptions, which has emerged as a central issue facing academic interlibrary loan. Best practices in the context of relations with commercial document delivery suppliers, budgeting, services to distance learning students, special collections, and measuring productivity and evaluating services also appear in the study.

The nine study participants were selected to represent a broad geographic diversity and for their reputations as leading academic research libraries. Several of the participants were invited by the editor to take part in the study, and others answered a call for participants posted on ILLiad-L. Participants completed a questionnaire written and designed by the editor; in some cases, participants were also interviewed. A number of the participants are members of the Association of Research Libraries, and all of the libraries participate in large resource sharing consortia.

Acknowledgments

The editor wishes to acknowledge and express gratitude to all of the participants in the study. The questionnaire was fairly time intensive, and many of the participants took time away from busy schedules to correspond with the editor by email or telephone. Their efforts and expertise has produced the present monograph.

Summary of Key Findings

The table below summarizes information for the case study participants and includes the number of students, library holdings, ARL (Association of Research Libraries) membership status, and the total number of items borrowed and loaned. With one exception, the participating ILL departments loaned more items than they borrowed, and three of the libraries borrowed approximately less than half of the number of items loaned. All of the libraries participating in the study hold over a million volumes in their respective collections; seven of the participating libraries each house two million or more volumes. Six of the libraries participating in the study are ARL members.

Participating University or College	Student Population	ARL Member	Library Holdings	Number of Items Borrowed and Loaned (fiscal/calendar year)
University of Texas at Arlington	25,000	No	Volumes: 1,181,950 Serials: 3,547 (print) 27,425 (electronic)	Borrowed: 13,848 Loaned: 14,394
Tulane University	11,157	Yes	Volumes: 3 million (print) Serials: 8,000	Borrowed: 6,573 Loaned: 12,210
University of Minnesota	66,099	Yes	Volumes: 6,800,000 (print) Serials: 77,000 (print and electronic)	Borrowed: 34,465 Loaned: 29,785
Indiana University-Purdue University Indianapolis	30,000	No	Volumes: 1,338,889 Serials: 36,000	Borrowed: 17,997 Loaned: 36,942
Brigham Young University	33,000	Yes	Items: 8 million (3.3 million books, 27,000 journals and additional materials)	Borrowed: 30,053 Loaned: 47,031
University of Tennessee	26,000	Yes	Volumes: 2.6 million	Borrowed: 20,815 Loaned: 30,453
Colorado State University	24,700	Yes	Volumes: 2 million serials: 31,300 (with access to 24,000 online journals)	Borrowed: 66,485 Loaned: 70,733
Oberlin College	2,800	No	Items: 2,352,985	Borrowed: 17,625 Loaned: 44,413
Stony Brook University	23,000	Yes	Volumes: 2 million (books) Serials: 63,000 (electronic journals)	Borrowed: 11,106 Loaned: 12,930

Description of Staffing, Continuing Education and ILL Budget

The table below provides summary data for the titles of the department head(s), titles and numbers of support staff and number of student assistants (when specified by the participant). Two of the participants identified themselves as professional librarians as part of their titles, one as an Access Services Head, one as Head of Resource Sharing and Document Delivery, with the remaining participants designating non-librarian titles with supervisory responsibilities. Most of the departments reported relying on student assistants for pulling and scanning materials and other tasks. Specific duties of department heads and staff are reported in detail in each case study.

University/College	Department Head(s)	Staff	Student Assistants
UT Arlington	ILL Manager	Library Assistants (5)	Student Assistants (5)
Tulane University	Head, Circulation and Interlibrary Loan	Library Technicians (3)	Student Workers (2-4)
University of Minnesota	Head, Interlibrary Loan, Borrowing (1), Library Manager, Lending (1)	Library Supervisor (1), Library Assistants (6.5)	Student Assistants
IUPUI	Interlibrary Loan Librarian	Interlibrary Services Senior Assistant (1), Interlibrary Loan Clerk (1)	Student Assistants (2.5-3)
Brigham Young University	Access Services Chair	Document Delivery Manager (1), ILL Supervisor (2), Document Delivery Supervisor (2), Copy Center Supervisor (2)	Student Workers (12.5)
University of Tennessee	Head, Resource Sharing and Document Delivery	Borrowing Supervisor, Borrowing Associates (2), Lending Supervisor, Lending Associate (1),	Student Workers
Colorado State University	Interlibrary Loan Coordinator	Borrowing Unit Head, Lending Unit Head, Support Staff (4)	Student Workers
Oberlin College	Interlibrary Loan Supervisor	N/A	Student Assistants (7)
Stony Brook University	Head, Interlibrary Loan and Business Librarian	Instructional Support Technician, Instructional Support Specialist, Library Clerks (3)	Student Workers

All of the interlibrary loan departments reported participating in formal and informal continuing education, both at the department head level and support staff level, when applicable. Examples include attendance at annual ILLiad conferences; regional resource sharing conferences sponsored by networks and consortia like TexShare, GWLA (Greater Western Library Alliance) and the MINITEX Library Information Network; and national ALA conferences.

Budget information varied in terms of annual costs and the budget categories presented by participants. Budget information is best interpreted contextually by the size of the library, volume of business, and local budget situation and is not easily summarized. Readers should refer to each case study for budget information.

Software and Automation

The libraries participating in the study universally use the OCLC ILLiad client as their automated system (the CSU Libraries report using ILLiad and Relais) to meet their resource sharing needs. All of the libraries use ILLiad to deliver articles electronically (either using Odyssey or posting Ariel/scanned PDFs) to their constituents. With its variety of applications to support and facilitate resource sharing, ILLiad has become the preferred standard for interlibrary loan departments among academic (and public) libraries. Several of the participants reported using ILLiad enhancements, such as Web Circulation, Odyssey Helper, and Trusted Sender. Others reported using the DOCLINE® and Rapid services with the ILLiad interface to request materials. Participants reported positive comments about using ILLiad and expressed overall satisfaction with the client.

Resource Sharing Consortia

Resource sharing consortia (or networks or systems) play an integral role in interlibrary loan services for all of the libraries surveyed. All of the case study respondents participate in more than one consortium, and all of the libraries report using consortia as their primary resource for obtaining ILL materials. Major cost savings, exceptionally quick turnaround time, convenient courier services, access to extensive holdings from member collections, reduced subscription rates and excellent service (resulting in high user satisfaction) are just some of the key advantages cited by libraries for participating in resource sharing consortia.

Examples of consortia cited by case study participants include SOLINET (Southeastern Library Network), KUDZU (Association of Southeastern Research Libraries' ILL Services Program), The Oberlin Group, OCLC/RLG SHARES, RapidILL, UALC (Utah Academic Library Consortium) and other statewide library consortia. Participation in multiple consortia has clearly emerged as a key best practice for interlibrary loan departments in academic libraries.

Commercial Document Delivery

Perhaps as a result of the advantages of consortial participation, all of the departments reported relatively low use of commercial document delivery services. The ILL departments routinely obtain materials for low or no cost through resource sharing consortia before resorting to commercial document delivery suppliers. Departments will use these suppliers only in certain cases; for example, if the material is not available from other lending libraries, if the constituent needs a high quality color copy or an article preprint, or if the request is needed immediately. Some of the libraries also purchase material from document delivery suppliers to avoid paying higher copyright royalties when use exceeds the CONTU "Rule of Five" guideline. Libraries report using commercial services on a case-by-case basis and prefer to order from the least expensive service available.

Libraries participating in this study purchase material from Ingenta, the British Library, Harvard Business Publishing, CISTI, ASME, Sage, Informa, NTIS, Storming Media, InfoTrieve, the National Library of Medicine and other document delivery service providers.

Copyright and Licensing

Limitations in licensing provisions for lending articles from electronic journals emerged as a major issue facing the libraries participating in the study. Most of the respondents expressed concern over these limitations. They emphasized the importance of obtaining lending rights to electronic journal subscriptions to provide optimal ILL services for their constituents. All of the libraries reported proactive and aggressive attempts on the part of electronic licensing and collection development librarians to negotiate lending rights for electronic subscriptions. ILL department heads reported strongly supporting these efforts but played a limited role in licensing negotiations. Several libraries, including the Oberlin Libraries and BYU, mentioned taking advantage of memberships in consortia as leverage for negotiating rights with publishers and vendors. The CSU Libraries reportedly will not sign licenses unless ILL is allowed.

More than one participant noted the importance of electronic resource management systems to track and provide licensing information to ILL departments.

Institutional Repositories and Open Access

Surprisingly, institutional repositories (IR) and open access (OA) materials have not substantially impacted interlibrary loan services, at least not for the libraries surveyed. Most of the participants report the same or an increased volume of business, and most of the departments do not have a system for tracking these materials. Because of time constraints, most respondents do not routinely conduct special searches for institutional repository or open access materials as part of their workflows, and rely largely on OPAC holding information to determine if these materials are available to patrons. One participant, the University of Minnesota Libraries, noted an increase in this type of material located by its staff, and Tulane

University reported borrowing less USPTO material. The IUPUI University Library searches Google Scholar for thesis/dissertation requests and conference papers before ordering from traditional resources. In general, the respondents reported minimal impact on services and workflow from IR/OA materials.

The notable exception is the Rapid (CSU) database for automatically searching and harvesting open access journal articles, which boasts a seven-minute average turnaround time. Two of the libraries, University of Tennessee Libraries and the IUPUI University Library, reported the benefits of access to these articles using the Rapid without having to search for this material.

Service Priorities for Constituents

All of the libraries report offering the same services (with some exceptions) to their constituents regardless of their status as students or faculty members. In general, the departments do not charge at all for services (some reported occasionally charging under special circumstances), and most do not impose limits on the amount of material patrons can order. Turnaround time and fill rates emerged as the top service priorities for departments participating in the study.

A number of interlibrary loan departments offer special services to their constituents. Some of the libraries reported special collection development services. The University of Texas at Arlington Libraries "Books on Demand" program, for example, allows staff to purchase title requests published in the current or previous year to permanently add to the collection. Such programs benefit constituents by providing access to needed material without imposing traditional ILL time constraints or having to order the same book through ILL for ongoing research. A number of the participants offer special document delivery services for constituents, delivering material held locally in their collections or traditional ILL requests, or both. Examples include the IUPUI University Library's Article Delivery Service, University of Tennessee Libraries' Library Express service, and document delivery services offered by the CSU Libraries, the Howard B. Lee Library (BYU) and the Stony Brook University Libraries. Requested articles are retrieved from journals in the collection, scanned and delivered electronically to faculty constituents (and students in some cases). In departments offering ILB delivery services, books are delivered and retrieved for patrons.

Services to Distance Learning Students

All of the departments offer the same ILL services to distance education students as to other constituents, with some minor differences. The distance education students sign up for ILLiad accounts and receive the majority of their articles electronically. Several libraries report sending books and other ILB material to students using their courier services, and distance education students are responsible for returning materials (the University of Texas at Arlington Libraries provides a postage-paid, return-mailing label). Almost all of the departments reported offering document delivery from local collections (articles and books) to distance education students (and the Stony Brook University Libraries will even provide document delivery to students doing fieldwork in remote locations).

More than one department reported problems with students identifying their status as distance education students in their ILLiad accounts. Two of the libraries, and the IUPUI University Library and the University of Tennessee Libraries, use their ILLiad system to flag DE requests for special handling. Several libraries reported recent increases in distance education requests.

Special Collections

The majority of the libraries typically do not loan special collections items or lend out such items only under special circumstances. Decisions to lend out items are made on a case-by-case basis by library staff working in special collections. Participants report that items housed in special collections are more likely to be photocopied or scanned than loaned to a borrowing library. In most cases, the departments will forward requests to special collections for consideration, and then work with special collections to send out requested materials. Materials are usually sent through UPS or FedEx for tracking purposes, and carefully packed for proper protection. In some cases, lending libraries require the borrowing library to follow special handling instructions or only allow the material to be used in the library's special collections room. Several of the participants report following the ACRL *Guidelines for the Interlibrary Loan of Rare and Unique Materials* for handling these requests.

Measuring Productivity and Evaluating Services

Most of the reporting libraries use turnaround time and fill rate as the chief measures for evaluating service and productivity. Depending on the library, departments run ILLiad reports weekly, monthly, annually or on an as-needed basis, and several libraries report using customized Microsoft Access reports to analyze data. Examples of other reports include orders submitted, requests cancelled, reports identifying frequent lenders and borrowers, patron demographics, CCC copyright reports and reports run for historical comparisons. Many reports are used to support collection development purchase decisions for monographs and journals. Statistics are used to establish benchmarks and to identify areas that need improvement, and for annual ARL reporting purposes. Libraries also report running and using reports for various consortia, and generating OCLC reports for IFM and other data.

Qualitative measures used by participants include ARL LibQual surveys, customer service surveys, Web questionnaires and feedback received in person or by email. In several cases, qualitative feedback resulted in new or enhanced ILL services, such as electronic document delivery for constituents.

University of Texas at Arlington

Rachel Robbins, Interlibrary Loan Manager,
University of Texas at Arlington Library

I. Description of the University of Texas at Arlington and Library

With a commitment to life-enhancing research, teaching excellence and service to the community, The University of Texas at Arlington is the educational leader in the heart of the Dallas-Fort Worth metroplex. Founded in 1895 as a private liberal arts institution, UT Arlington achieved senior college status in 1959 and became part of The University of Texas System in 1965. The University's nearly 25,000 students pursue more than 180 bachelor's, master's and doctoral degrees in an extensive range of disciplines. Of UT Arlington's 125,000 alumni, 88,000 live in North Texas. Their presence helps the University create an annual economic impact of $1 billion on the region.

The University of Texas at Arlington Library promotes learning, teaching and research to enrich the intellectual, creative and professional growth of students and faculty. The UT Arlington Library collection includes over 1,181,950 volumes (on shelves), access to 235,399 e-Books, 3,547 print serial subscriptions and 27,425 electronic serial subscriptions. The UT Arlington Library employs 48 professional and 80 support staff and is open 142 hours weekly. The UT Arlington Library offers the best choice for navigating the world of ideas.

In 2007/2008, the UT Arlington Library borrowed 13,848 items and loaned 14,394 items to other libraries.

II. Description of Staffing and ILL Budget

The following staff comprise the ILL department at the University of Texas at Arlington Library: Ms. Rachel Robbins, ILL Manager, Library Assistant IV; Library Assistant II, Lending Manager; Library Assistant II, Lending and Floater; Library Assistant II, Borrowing Orderer; Library Assistant II, Borrowing Processor; and five Student Assistants.

The ILL Manager prepares reports; works on difficult requests; resolves problems about wrong materials sent or items lost; reviews procedure and policy; implements changes in services; makes minor changes to the ILL Web site; helps with ordering in general; hires, trains and supervises staff; and suggests purchase of software and hardware related to ILL.

The Library Assistant II, Lending Manager, is the primary lender; manages daily work flow, lending student employees, billing, problem resolution, mail wrapping for the entire ILL operation; and provides ILL customer service.

The Library Assistant II, Lending and Floater, assists the lending manager with whatever tasks need to be accomplished, acts as back up when the primary lender is gone is a floater to help with other tasks as assigned (in particular covering the circulation desk) and provides ILL customer service.

The Library Assistant II, Borrowing Orderer, fills in as ILL Manager as needed, supervises borrowing students, does the bulk of borrowing orders and helps with problem citations, provides ILL customer service, processes received materials as needed and assists with technical issues.

The Library Assistant II, Borrowing Processor, processes received materials, handles overdues, sends invoices through for payment, oversees the opening and distribution of all ILL mail, does renewals and returns and provides ILL customer service.

Student Assistants working in Borrowing process paper and electronic articles received, help with opening mail, and do simple ordering and some data input. Student Assistants in Lending pull materials, wrap materials for shipping, scan materials for electronic delivery and make photocopies.

Staff Education

All ILL department staff at the University of Texas at Arlington Library are encouraged to take advantage of locally offered training programs that range anywhere from computing to customer service skills and wellness programs. Staff have been allowed to attend TexShare and other ILL conferences within the state as well as the ILLiad Conference at Virginia Beach and to participate in training sessions offered by Amigos Library Services. "Right now we are looking into the annual training membership with ILLiad. It would allow us access to all their online training materials, which staff could use at their convenience," says Robbins. "All in all, the library administration is very supportive of staff training monetarily, as well as with leave time."

Placement of ILL Department in Library's Organization

Interlibrary Loan falls under the auspices of Access Services with the ILL Manager reporting to the head of Access Services. According to Robbins, "Until May of this year, Lending was performed by a team known as the Internal Materials Group and Borrowing was performed by a team known as the External Materials Group. This split in the ILL functions happened about 10 years ago with an organizational restructuring; however, we are glad to have them back together."

Budget Information

"Not much of the ILL budgeting is separated out from the rest of Access Services," explains Robbins, "so equipment and supplies get lumped with the rest of the department. Two figures that are tracked separately are postage and document delivery charges."

For the academic year 2007-2008 the department spent $21,000 mailing ILL packages. $81,400 was budgeted for a line item called "document delivery services," although that title is not particularly accurate. That fund includes royalty payments on reserve items, royalty payments on ILL items and charges paid out to other libraries and document suppliers for interlibrary loan activity.

For 2007-2008, approximately $137,000 was spent on five staff salaries. Approximately $4,000 (approximately 2,200 hours) was spent on student employees mostly at a work-study rate.

Best Management Advice for Other Academic ILL Departments

Robbins offers the following management advice for other ILL departments to make the best use of their budgets:
- Electronically deliver materials, invoices and overdue notifications as much as possible.
- Give the manager a credit card to purchase items as needed (you have to weigh staff time saved and customer service against amount spent).
- Use an ILL management system like ILLiad or Clio.
- Make full use of staffing options (we have Access Services 3rd shift staff – the ones that keep us open in the wee hours of the morning – process much of our borrowing returns).
- Participate in the OCLC IFM program to cut down on your accounts receivable and accounts payable work; participation in ILL reciprocal agreements like Amigos and LVIS are also good options for the same reason.
- Cross training between lending and borrowing staff and students
- Participate in a consortial courier service if that option is available to you; participation in TExpress saves us considerable shipping costs between Texas libraries.
- Bubble wrap mailers are cheaper than gray matter mailers both from a supply standpoint and a shipping standpoint (they are lighter in weight, so can save you a little in postage cost, too).
- Use a company that allows you to comparison shop for the best shipping rate for special items; we use eShipGlobal which compares costs between UPS, DHL and FedEx, so we can choose the best rate.

III. Software and Automation

The University of Texas at Arlington Library relies on OCLC's ILLiad and uses it for three functions: interlibrary loan (lending and borrowing), a pull and deliver service for UT Arlington faculty (called Faculty Resource Delivery) and document delivery to distance education and disabled students. These services are not all performed by ILL staff. FRD and document delivery are performed by others.

The department uses Odyssey and Ariel and Adobe Professional for electronic document delivery.

- ✍ Lending: "For any articles we are allowed to send as electronic documents through the licensing agreements, we send them via Ariel or as a PDF attachment to an email," Robbins explains. "For articles we photocopy from our paper collection, we send them electronically via Ariel if we are allowed. We will fax or mail as our last options to fill requests. We had difficulties getting Odyssey going for lending so we do not use it currently, but plan to do that when things slow down again."
- ✍ Borrowing: 'We receive articles via both Odyssey and Ariel. Articles we receive in electronic format we store on our ILLiad server for patrons to pick up. If we receive an article in paper format and we are allowed to scan it and deliver it to the patron electronically we do so. Many libraries," states Robbins, "choose to send us electronic articles via an email attachment or have us go pick up our article off their Web server."

Recent Software and Automation Enhancements

The ILL department recently purchased an additional scanner to avoid having lending and borrowing competing for time on the same equipment.

Best Management Advice for Other Academic ILL Departments

Robbins states, "Having started with ILL in the Dark Ages (actually more like the Middle Ages - 1982), electronic delivery is awesome both from the supplier's and the receiver's standpoint. And electronic notification using email is indispensable. Gone are the days we employed a student to simply be on the phone calling patrons to let them know their material is here. Our patrons love the ILLiad Web user interface since it now allows them to check the status of their request, renew materials themselves and get a list of items they have requested in the past."

IV. Resource Sharing Consortia

The University of Texas at Arlington Library participates in ILL agreements with Amigos, Amigos/BCR and LVIS. The library is also a member of TexShare, academic and public libraries in Texas who work together for special services like shared databases.

Robbins has noticed that the courier service (called TExpress) serving participating libraries, part of the TexShare program, saves their department considerable shipping costs for interlibrary loan activity and, depending on the locale, can be quicker than U.S. Mail. However, since TExpress has expanded to Amigos libraries outside the state of Texas, (a service known as TransAmigos) delivery time between libraries has visibly increased. TExpress allows Robbins to save postage, but the department no longer gets as great a benefit in turnaround time. On the plus side, Robbins has seen less loss or damage to materials than with materials sent via U.S. mail.

Says Robbins, "The more full text electronic databases TexShare can purchase on behalf of our patrons the better."

V. Commercial Document Delivery

Robbins outlines the following cases in which their ILL department decides to make use of a document delivery service provider:

- ✍ If the request is not filled in our first round of ILL requests, we check our options to see if a document supplier is available. This is primarily to keep our turnaround time down in the interest of customer service.
- ✍ If the patron indicates that they need a really good, clean and/or color electronic copy because of highly detailed and/or technical drawings, we may try a document provider first.
- ✍ If the item is only available from a document supplier; for example, Harvard Business Cases, publication preprints, e-journals.
- ✍ If it is easier to get from a document supplier than to play the hunt-and-peck game to see who has it.
- ✍ Obscure foreign journals unavailable in the U.S.
- ✍ When we want to pay royalties up front (say, we have reached our limit of five on a title and the title is not a participant in the CCC).
- ✍ The publisher Alibris has attached their holdings to OCLC records and set up billing through IFM on OCLC. We use Alibris when we have been unable to borrow a title from another library and can purchase it for a reasonable price. Once the ILL patron is done with the book, we pass it along to collection development so they can decide if it should be added to the collection or not.
- ✍ We use ProQuest to provide electronic dissertations to our patrons. While patrons can access ProQuest electronic holdings themselves, we still see a lot of requests come through ILL borrowing. (In September 2008 we handled 66 of these.) In addition, for those items not available through ProQuest, we provide patrons unbound paper copies of dissertations through Dissertation Express for a special rate of $29 per item.

The University of Texas at Arlington Library uses the following document delivery service providers: Ingenta, CISTI, British Library, AIAA, ASCE, ASME, Blackwell Synergy, Caliber, Document Store, Inderscience, Informa, Highwire Press, Japanese Science and Technology Agency, Metapress, Minerva Medica, MIT Press, NTIS, NLM, Oxford Journals, UMI, Proquest (Electronic Dissertations), Routledge, Sage, Springerlink, Taylor Francis, Thieme Connect, Wiley Interscience, Yale Info Technology Service and Dissertation Express.

According to Robbins, "We generally go with the document delivery service provider we can find who can supply it at a reasonable cost."

Unmediated or Mediated Access to Document Delivery Services

Robbins says, "We have provided unmediated use of Ingenta to faculty for several years, but it has been underutilized so we will probably stop that after this year. We opened it up to graduate students as well and offered training for it, but it never really took off. We do have a cost limit per article imposed by the system so that if it was above that cost, they would have to request it through ILL or have a staff member override that limit."

"We have a pretty generous library administration in terms of a budget for ILL and document supply," adds Robbins. "They are willing to budget for these expenses in the name of customer service. So any stoppage of a request due to cost or decision to pass the charge on to the patron is generally decided by the ILL Manager or in the special cases, in a dialogue between the ILL Manager and the department head. We have seen an improvement in both fill rate and turnaround time since our administration has taken this approach. We have been tracking costs paid to document suppliers for ILL materials for four to five years now."

Library Fee-Based Services

The University of Texas at Arlington Library does not offer a document delivery service that competes with other commercial suppliers. The department does borrow from other libraries that charge fees for their services. The library has a special agreement with the University of Texas at Austin (the biggest of the University of Texas schools) for copy delivery service, which the department uses extensively. UT Austin charges $8 per article and usually delivers the items electronically within 24-36 hours. In September 2008 UT Austin filled over 250 article requests for the UT Arlington ILL department.

Best Management Advice for Other Academic ILL Departments

"Go to the ones that can provide you with an electronic copy if possible…" Robbins suggests, "but be sure to read the fine print as some providers specifically say their copy is not to be used for interlibrary loan."

VI. Copyright and Licensing

ILL Copyright-Compliant Policy or Guidelines

Robbins has her staff follow the CONTU "Rule of Five" guideline and report any articles requested over five (published within the last five years) and pay royalties. The department uses the copyright feature in ILLiad to track the articles "over five" throughout the year. Ordering staff use that feature to check each new copy request against titles already ordered throughout the year. If copyright needs to be reported, it goes into the queue to be reported when staff are ready.

"We have been reporting copyright on an annual basis," Robbins reports, "but this year hope to start reporting more frequently. This will prevent our budget from being hit with such a high one-time charge each year. We have the Copyright Clearance Center bill us and we pay that invoice with a check."

Best Management Advice for Other Academic ILL Departments

Robbins advises other ILL departments to:

- ✍ Make sure your collection development people are getting information on what you are paying in royalties on what titles. They can be your best allies in addressing frequently requested titles.
- ✍ Have a credit card for ILL purposes. If you hit your limit of five on a title that is not cleared with the CCC, you might be able to order the item from a document supplier who covers royalties with the costs.

Electronic Licensing Agreements for Lending

"Some subscriptions include licensing provisions for lending and others do not," states Robbins. When negotiating contracts, our librarians try to negotiate as liberal an agreement as they can get (for what they can afford)." Robbin's ILL staff has no official role to play in licensing strategies for the library.

Major ILL Copyright and Licensing Issues

"In terms of borrowing, as far as our patrons are concerned, they would like all copies they order through interlibrary loan delivered to them electronically; unfortunately, licensing does not always allow us to do that," Robbins explains.

"Licensing for our databases is extremely important to lending. We provide lots of articles each day through our databases, when licensing allows," Robbins adds.

The Lending Manager has a close relationship with the UT Arlington licensing librarian in acquisitions to help identify what the department is allowed to supply through interlibrary loan. For a long time the department turned away any request that was part of the UT Arlington electronic collections. Changing this has greatly improved the library's lending fill rate, but is certainly more labor intensive for the department. The transmission of these materials is via Ariel, fax, mail or e-mail. Ariel serves as a good transmission vehicle since it means quick service in an electronic format for the customer although it is not always without problems. Many articles do not transmit and have to be resent. Fax and mail are last resorts, but there are databases used by the department that will only allow this type of delivery. Robbins finds sending a PDF as an email attachment is the most reliable method of transmission. The impact for lending is that the more databases used by the department, the better the results are for filling requests. Scanning from paper copies can be very time consuming, more labor intensive and more prone to follow-up problems (missing pages, bad scan or wrong article copied).

VII. Institutional Repositories and Open Access

Obtaining Materials from Open Access Journals or Institutional Repositories

The ILL department does not currently check institutional repositories before ordering articles…"although we may at some point in the not too distant future," says Robbins. "What we are doing is ordering borrowing requests through regular ILL means (OCLC). If it comes back unfilled after the first round of libraries, the ILL Manager searches the Web to see if it is available for free or from a document supplier or other source and we get the item that way." When searching problem citation requests, staff will sometimes locate the item in an open access format and will forward it to the patron or provide the patron with the Web address. "It is a bit embarrassing, but nice (because they are doing our work for us), to request an article through regular ILL means and have the lender conditional [editor: correct?] us back that the item is available from open access…."

ILL staff rely on their OPAC to identify open access journal articles. When searching problem requests, staff will sometimes identify these items through a Google search.

The department does not keep separate stats for these sorts of materials. "When we can," Robbins says, "we save the file as a PDF on our ILLiad server and the patron 'picks it up' the same way they access their other ILL electronic articles. If, for some reason, we cannot do a PDF, we refer the patron to the Web page."

Impact of Open Access Publications, Institutional Repositories, or Low Cost Archives

These types of material have not had much of an impact on the UT Arlington Library Interlibrary Loan Department yet, but Robbins expects that will change with time. "Open access publications can make us look good though," admits Robbins. "For example, our assistant director received an email from a faculty member who rather desperately needed an article for a presentation (why they went to her instead of ILL, we don't know). Our assistant director forwarded the email to ILL and told the faculty member we would get back with her. We found the article via open access and the faculty member was emailed the article less than half an hour after she initially contacted our assistant director. Both the faculty member and the assistant director were duly impressed."

VIII. Service Priorities for Constituents

The UT Arlington Library ILL Department generally treats all our ILL customers equally with no patron getting precedence over another because of their status. Requests are processed on a first-come, first-served basis. The library does not limit the number of requests a patron can submit. If someone submits many requests at one time, staff might batch them and order several each day to avoid favoring one person's requests at the expense of others. The department will *very rarely* pass on charges for interlibrary loan to the patron and get their approval of those charges in advance[editor: do they get approval or not?]. Except for textbooks for classes, the department tries to borrow materials through interlibrary loan for their constituents.

ILL Services for Community Members, Visiting Scholars or Other Institutions

Generally, the library does not provide services to community members, visiting scholars or other institutions; there are two exceptions:

- ✍ The library will continue to provide service to retired faculty and staff as long as the university gives them a valid UT Arlington ID and password.
- ✍ If visiting scholars are given a valid UT Arlington ID and password, then the library will provide ILL service to them as well. The department that the visiting scholar works with is responsible for setting that up.

Special Services to Constituents

Two years ago the ILL department started the Books on Demand Program. If any ILL patron turns in a request for a book published in the current or previous year, ILL staff will evaluate the request for consideration for the library to purchase. Essentially the library is using ILL as a collection development tool. What happens is this:

- The patron puts in the ILL order.
- If the book was published in the current year or last, ILL staff moves it to a special request queue.
- ILL staff look at the request to see if it meets established criteria (i.e., that we do not own it already, it is available domestically, costs less than $150, is not a textbook or workbook, is in English, is scholarly in nature and in print).
- If the item meets those criteria, the request is forwarded to acquisitions, which orders it.
- When the book comes in, it goes to the ILL patron first to use for six weeks and when it is returned it is added to the collection.

"We have found the majority of books get here in the same amount of time that an interlibrary loaned book does," says Robbins. "Also, we found that, once added to the collection, these titles are being used again by others."

The ILL department does not routinely interview patrons to determine the need for requests, and since patrons can "only" submit requests via the ILLiad Web interface [editor: clarify] (and staff do not have the face-to-face contact with people as they place orders). However, interviews might follow the placement of requests if the requests are difficult, unique or confusing.

Notification and Delivery of Materials

The ILL department gives its patrons the option to be notified via phone or email. Most choose email. For copied materials, three options are offered:

- electronic delivery, when possible.
- hold the material for pick up at the 1st floor circulation desk of the Central Library (ILL is open 24/5 so patrons can pick it up at their convenience).
- mail it to a home address or office.

For loanables, (unless it is something designated as "library use only"), the department asks that patrons pick it up at the Central Library unless they are a distance education student or faculty. In which case, we will then mail the item to them via courier and enclose a postage-paid return label to cover the expense when they mail it back.

IX. Services to Distance Learning Students

"We are getting more ILL requests from distance education students," reports Robbins.

"Generally requests for copies are not a problem since we can mail or electronically deliver the copies. Loans can be more problematic. We courier the ILL item to the student with a postage-paid, return-mailing label. Getting the loans back in a timely manner seems to be most problematic and we have had a case with two books (one belonging to the British Lending Library) we wound up paying for."

Robbins believes their biggest problem is identifying the distance education students, since they often do not put this information into their ILL profile when they create it online. It is not unusual for staff to contact the patron to let them know their item is in and then they will call or email ILL with the message that they expected the item delivered. Once ILL has that information, it is added to the profile, so staff will know how to handle future transactions. ILL plans to revise the Web page to more easily glean that information.

Special Services for Distance Education Constituents

The distance education students (and special needs students for that matter) can request materials to be delivered to them from the library's collections. This is facilitated through the ILL system (ILLiad) although it is not handled by the same staff. The process is:

- ✍ Students place their request through ILLiad.
- ✍ ILL staff search the request and if we do not own it, we order it.
- ✍ If staff find the item in the collections, the request is moved to a distance education processing queue.
- ✍ That staff handles pulling and copying or checking out and delivery.
- ✍ If the item cannot be found or is checked out, the request is moved back to the ILL queue with a note and staff order it from another provider.

"We only see a small percentage of those students using our document delivery services," Robbins says. "The work is handled by one part-time staff, and it does not keep her busy 20 hours a week so she has other responsibilities as well. Nursing students are by far the heaviest users of this service since our School of Nursing has at least five satellite programs in Texas. We do not charge for any of our delivery services (ILL, DE, special needs, or Faculty Resource Delivery). The costs are largely covered by our Student Library Use Fee."

Partnerships with Other Libraries to Serve Distance Education Constituents

The TexShare library card is used by almost all academic and public libraries in the state. Distance education students (as well as other patrons) can apply for that card online and it will be mailed to them. They then present that card to the library at which they want privileges. Loan policies and restrictions are set by each library. Participating libraries and their policies are accessible on the TexShare Web site which is maintained by the Texas State Library.

X. Special Collections

"Right now interlibrary loan does not provide any services for copying materials from our special collections," states Robbins. "Our special collections/ILL policies have not been looked at in many, many years and that is something we will be meeting about later this month to review. So right now if someone wants copies of anything from special collections, they have to work with that department directly."

"We have a couple collections on microfilm that we will lend out, but we do require that the borrower return the material insured. The collections are Texas county records (which we technically do not own as they are officially property of the Texas State Library) and the Yucatan Collection (which are older documents from that area of the world). Both collections get reasonably good usage…the county records more so than the Yucatan."

Affect of Digital Special Collections on Traditional ILL

According to Robbins, a few materials are now available on the library's Web site that outsiders can access without having to work through interlibrary loan or special collections staff. All of these are items that would not have been available through traditional interlibrary loan and items they would have had to work with special collections to obtain or come in and use on site.

XI. Measuring Productivity and Evaluating Services

The department runs a monthly report (as well as an annual report) for the department head. Department staff look at activity for the month: requests received and requests filled for borrowing and lending, format (returnables or nonreturnables), turnaround time and reasons for items not filled, to list a few examples. The department also compares requests at the same time the previous year to see if they are up or down. This information is particularly useful in identifying trends that might impact staff or student budgets.

ILL staff uses ILLiad for the monthly and annual statistics and sometimes manipulates ILLiad data in Access for nontypical statistical information. For example, a faculty member requested that the library purchase a microfilm collection that cost thousands of dollars. Acquisitions asked for the order history data to ascertain if ordering through ILL within the scope of that collection justified the cost of purchasing the collection. OCLC statistics are used for IFM data. ILLiad is used for copyright report generation along with an access report, and we generate an annual report for the Books on Demand program.

"At any time, collection development personnel can access ILLiad to find titles more frequently requested for consideration to add to the collection," says Robbins. "They have been particularly proactive in purchasing journals for which we have received a high number of ILL requests. When we pass along our copyright report to collection development, we include royalties paid to help them evaluate if it would be better to purchase rather than get through ILL and pay copyright fees."

Other Tools Used to Evaluate Productivity and Service

Robbins reports that the library has used LibQual twice in the past few years and, fortunately, comments on ILL are generally "glowing" and thus, unfortunately, not providing much feedback that staff can react to/improve upon. "Probably one of the most productive tools we have," she says, "is the feedback we get from our patrons as we handle their requests…particularly 'problem' requests.

"We try to be proactive and if a suggestion is identified as sensible, easy and inexpensive, we do it," says Robbins. "Suggestions that will be more timely or costly to implement generally have to get moved to slower times like the Christmas holidays or summer, although we do not see as much of a lull as we did in the past."

"Statistics helped us justify the movement of a staff position from borrowing to lending this year," Robbins relates, "and patron feedback led us to deliver documents electronically as much as licensing/copyright will allow; we are currently investigating alternate means to borrow films for students since the demand for this format through interlibrary loan has greatly increased this last year."

Tulane University

**Hayden Battle, Head of Circulation and Interlibrary Loan Services,
Howard-Tilton Memorial Library**

I. Description of Tulane University and Library

Tulane University is one of the most highly regarded and selective independent research universities in the United States. A member of the prestigious Association of American Universities, Tulane is proud to be a part of this select group of 62 universities with pre-eminent programs of graduate and professional education and scholarly research. Tulane's schools and colleges offer undergraduate, graduate and professional degrees in the liberal arts, science and engineering, architecture, business, law, social work, medicine and public health and tropical medicine. Tulane strives to connect its values and mission to the needs of the city of New Orleans, the state of Louisiana and the nation. Community involvement is now more important than ever as the university participates in the rebirth of New Orleans. Faculty and staff lend their expertise to rebuilding efforts and students gain real-world experience while putting their skills to use in the community.

Howard-Tilton Memorial Library is Tulane University's main library and supports undergraduate and graduate programs in the humanities, social sciences, and science and engineering. Its unique collections in areas such as Latin American studies, jazz and New Orleans history draw researchers from around the globe. The library houses more than 3 million print volumes, more than 8,000 current serials and invests more than $1.7 million a year in its digital collections of resources such as full text databases and online journals. Special collections include the Latin American Library, one of the world's principal collections for Latin American studies; the Hogan Jazz Archive; Manuscripts; Rare Books; University Archives; and the Southeastern Architectural Archive. The Architecture Library is located on the second floor of Richardson Memorial Hall. Tulane's libraries are ranked among the top 120 research libraries in North America.

The ILL department processed borrowing 8,083 [editor: 8,083 borrowing requests?] requests (6,573 were filled), and lending received 23,878 requests (12,210 were filled) for fiscal year [editor: 2008?].

II. Description of Staffing and ILL Budget

Howard-Tilton Memorial Library employs three full-time Library Technicians (one each in charge of lending and borrowing, and one responsible for electronic reserves and mail). In addition, the department shares a Library Technician with another department, whose responsibilities include receiving items from other libraries. The department employs two to four student workers. The Head of Circulation and Interlibrary Loan supervises library technicians.

Library Technician, Lending: Responsible for all aspects of lending, all of OCLC requests through ILLiad; she and students go to stacks to pull journals and books; she processes requests through ILLiad; oversees Ariel, processing/scanning; boxes books to send through mail or courier (LANTER delivery service). Supervises all student workers.

Library Technician, Borrowing: Responsible for processing requests using ILLiad; uses OCLC to select libraries that hold items and requests them; in charge of receiving process; notifies patrons to pick up material; processes electronic delivery for articles; and uses ILLiad to post Ariel articles as PDFs on the Web; monitors and answers departmental email. The borrowing technician deals with any problems patrons have, in person or on the phone.

Library Technician (shared with electronic reserves): Works with e-reserves; oversees billing through ILLiad; handles overdue or lost books; and assists the lending technician in getting materials ready to go out to mail through LANTER delivery service.

Student Workers (two-four each semester): Students work 10-20 hours a week, usually helping with the lending duties, going to stacks pulling books, scanning journal articles using Ariel and boxing up books.

Staff Education

"We have had specialized training in the past for various improvements to the OCLC ILLiad system, when those improvements were implemented," Battle reports. "For example, when the billing module changed, staff participated in an OCLC (Atlas system) training Webinar, and we received training with overhead scanning. Staff receive training whenever significant upgrades occur."

Battle attended the 2005 OCLC conference in Ohio and will attend the International ILLiad Conference conducted by Atlas Systems next year in Virginia Beach.

Staff members are also allowed to take part in university-led continuing education.

Placement of ILL Department in Library's Organization

Howard-Tilton Circulation and Interlibrary Loan Services Department is a combined department and falls under the public services division. The public services division includes government documents, reference services, music and other public service departments, and all report to the head of public services.

Role of Staff in Collection Development or Permanent Acquisitions

The ILL department provides information on an annual basis to the collections development group on all requested items. Staff query the ILLiad database and provide collection development librarians with lists of monographs and articles (with journal title, year and other bibliographic information), with departmental affiliation of faculty or student major. Data is presented in Excel format so that developers can sort information easily. The group uses this data to determine demand for future areas of collection development. Collection developers have used ILL data as a guide for purchasing more monographs in certain areas and more science journals. "The ILL department is willing to run specialized reports for selectors whenever they need them," says Battle.

Budget Information

The approximate budget is $105,000, with most of that going to salaries. In addition to staff salaries, the largest amount is spent on equipment upkeep. This approximate budget does not include any document delivery costs, or OCLC related fees or subscriptions.

Best Management Advice for other Academic ILL Departments

Battle advises other libraries to make use of interlibrary loan consortia, since they are cost effective. "The vast majority of our ILL activity is with the KUDZU or LOUIS (the inter-Louisiana consortium) and is therefore free except for membership fees," she states. "This greatly cuts down on per-item costs."

III. Software and Automation

"At our ILL office, everything is run off the OCLC ILLiad system," says Battle. "ILLiad has been in use since 2002 at Tulane. We currently run ILLiad off of our own server, located in the library."

For borrowing, patrons log on to the Web site and place orders via the ILLiad system. Staff then screens all photocopy requests for copyright compliance and places all requests through the ILLiad OCLC interface. Any requests held by Howard-Tilton Memorial Library are cancelled, and an email notification is sent to the constituent.

Once a loan arrives, it is received through ILLiad, and an e-mail notification is sent to the patron by the system. Articles are usually received via Ariel. The ILL staff uses ILLiad to sort these Ariel requests and place them on the Web as PDFs for Tulane patrons to access.

For lending, requests are downloaded by ILLiad to the server. "Our lending technician searches each request in our catalog to see if we own it and can lend it," Battle reports. "Once we have a searchable list, we print out each request on a search slip and send student workers to find the materials. Books are packed up and shipped out daily, either by mail or courier. Articles are scanned using an overhead scanner and Ariel software, and sent to Ariel addresses provided by the lending libraries. Books returned are checked in using the ILLiad system, then sent to the Circulation Desk for processing."

Best Management Advice for other Academic ILL Departments

"Currently, I would consider it essential to have ILLiad or a similar software program to run ILL," advises Battle. "In addition to Ariel or Odyssey, it allows a limited staff to service a relatively large patron base. Using these tools, we are able to present to our patrons a variety of options for getting materials, including the very popular electronic delivery for articles. Although staffing does not currently allow it, we also have the tools already to begin offering delivery of articles that we own here to faculty on campus. I have used ILLiad in various institutions for nine years and continue to be impressed with its power and versatility. Anyone looking to improve efficiency in their department should use it."

IV. Resource Sharing Consortia

Howard-Tilton Memorial Library is a member of SOLINET (Southeastern Library Network), KUDZU (Association of Southeastern Research Libraries' ILL Services Program) and CRL (Center for Research Libraries). The library is also a member of LOUIS (The Louisiana Library Network), a consortium of Louisiana libraries. LOUIS and KUDZU libraries run a daily courier service between the libraries of those consortia.

The KUDZU consortium includes a couple of dozen SOLINET members, and Tulane's SOLINET fee also covers participation in KUDZU. According to Battle, "We mostly get resources using KUDZU from the University of Tennessee, from Mississippi, the University of Miami, and the University of Kentucky. KUDZU is generally the fastest consortium and has the widest range of material since so many major ARL libraries participate. Our SOLINET fee allows us to borrow from KUDZU for free or at a reduced cost."

Howard-Tilton Memorial Library also pays a fee to participate in LOUIS, and borrowing and lending is then free among LOUIS libraries, which comprise most major libraries in Louisiana. Both KUDZU and LOUIS use the LANTER Delivery Service.

"Being a member of a consortium allows us to get a greater number of items more quickly for our patrons," adds Battle. "Since we have been using KUDZU, our fill-rate has greatly increased. Using KUDZU and LOUIS specifically, we have been able to take advantage of a courier, rather than having to pay mail rates."

The library loans a lot of material to other libraries through LOUIS and KUDZU. "Tulane is a much bigger lender than borrower," relates Battle. "We net lend about double what we borrow."

The ILL department also occasionally uses CRL for borrowing. "There are cases where a researcher will need 20 years of a newspaper. Unlike most educational libraries that wouldn't send that much, CRL will send boxes of microfilm and huge volumes of bound journals," Battle says. "The loan period is usually two to three months."

Best Management Advice of Other Academic ILL Departments

"ILLiad has made placing orders with members of our consortia much easier and faster," Battle summarizes. "By utilizing Ariel software, we can sometimes order and receive article requests that same day, and since we have reciprocal agreements within the consortium, those requests are much cheaper as well."

V. Commercial Document Delivery

"We have never been a big customer of document delivery, so its impact has not been very great," says Battle. "We did more in the past with engineering, [editor: the Engineering dept.?] which has been cut back after Katrina, and we also used to get a lot of dissertations and patents, but since these have gone digital, we don't need to buy them anymore. Howard-Tilton Memorial Library also has a strong journal collection, and since Katrina there's been a big push to purchase more electronic journals."

The decision to use a document delivery service is case-by case. "We will make special cases for faculty and specific types of requests, for example, foreign patents or dissertations," Battle says. "We have used Ingenta and CISTI in the past, and have also used ASM International. We make a choice for document delivery based upon who owns the item."

Unmediated or Mediated Access to Document Delivery Services

Ingenta is not provided for unmediated use by faculty. According to Battle, "Document delivery is mediated by the ILL staff. We have never had so great a demand for document delivery, so the question of limits has never come up. Document delivery is so rarely used that it is not tracked and has little impact on the budget."

Fee-Based Services

Howard-Tilton Memorial Library does not provide article lending for a fee in competition with commercial suppliers and does not borrow from libraries charging these fees.

VI. Copyright and Licensing

ILL Copyright-compliant Policy or Guidelines

The ILL department uses the "Rule of Five" guideline for items falling under copyright compliance. "The ILLiad system keeps track of this for us," reports Battle. "Every photocopy request is checked against a list of titles that we have five or more copies for the year. For payment, we go through the CCC. This system has worked very well for us so far, and I would recommend it to others."

Howard-Tilton Memorial Library Interlibrary Loan staff do not play a role in the library's licensing strategies.

Major ILL Copyright and Licensing Issues

Copyright is of major importance to ILL. According to Battle, "The most important aspect of copyright and licensing is access. For electronic journals, many institutions are not allowed to share articles via ILL and that limits access to potential patrons. While the Internet has allowed for increased sharing and borrowing, it has also placed severe restrictions on the types of materials we can borrow and how much we can get for our patrons."

"A lot of agreements with electronic journals specifically prevent them from sending these to other libraries through ILL, and many libraries have cancelled their print versions," adds Battle. "This has the potential to have a detrimental affect on ILL. Tulane tries to negotiate ILL lending options with electronic journal purchases, but many of the electronic subscriptions are not available for ILL."

VII. Institutional Repositories and Open Access

For ILL use, open access publications have had limited effect. "We check for items held at our library when OCLC indicates that we own it, which does not always include open access documents. The only time we do an in-depth search for a request is if it is particularly hard-to-find. To my knowledge, we have never searched an author's preprint in any open access database."

Battle doesn't think borrowing or lending have decreased overall due to open access journals or institutional repositories. Patents, however, are not borrowed as much, since the inception of the USPTO Open Access Web site.

II. Service Priorities for Constituents

"We have no difference in policies for undergraduates, graduates or faculty members. Everyone gets a three-week loan period with an optional two-week renewal, depending on the lending library's conditions," Battle states.

ILL Services for Community Members, Visiting Scholars or Other Institutions

Howard-Tilton Memorial Library offers ILL services only for faculty, staff and students affiliated with Tulane University.

Special Services to Constituents

The ILL department has sent articles through the mail in the past and will do this on a case-by-case basis as requested. Patrons can also come in to the ILL office if they require help or have special needs. Most patrons place orders via the Web page and do not require special help.

Notification and Delivery of Materials

Patrons receive an email notification automatically generated through the ILLiad client, or phone call notification of arriving materials. "For articles we receive electronically, most are now made available on the Web for our patrons to download," comments Battle. "If borrowing receives an article in paper over fax or in the mail, or the patron has requested a paper copy (patrons are given the option to only accept articles in print) then these are printed out and placed in Circulation. Books are placed behind the Circulation Desk for retrieval."

IX. Services to Distance Learning Students

"We service a relatively small number of distance students, based out of our Biloxi campus (probably no more than two or three dozen)," Battle reports. "Of that student body, we do not get a lot of requests each year. We do not charge anyone, including distance education students, for ILL services."

Biloxi students sign up for ILLiad accounts like regular students. Electronic copies of articles are available through ILLiad. Tulane University also runs a special courier twice a week to Biloxi, and materials can be sent to Biloxi students. "We do not service a large number of distance education students," Battle says. "With such a small demand, we have not had to alter services recently." Distance education requests are dealt with the same as regular requests.

"We are a member of SOLINET and the OCLC Reciprocal Borrowing consortium, which allows Tulane students and faculty, if out of state, to borrow materials on site from other member libraries," says Battle.

X. Special Collections

Tulane University has a large special collections department housed in a separate building. The ILL department refers requests to the special collections department, and "it's up to special collections if they want to photocopy or lend material," says Battle. "If they lent a book, they would work with lending to send out through ILLiad (since special collections is not set up with ILLiad). This is a rare occurrence, and lending is able to work with them on a case-to-case basis." Lending would arrange for any special packing and send the material out through FedEx or UPS."

In some cases, Howard-Tilton Memorial will have a circulating copy of an item in special collections, which can be loaned to another library.

XI. Measuring Productivity and Evaluating Services

The ILL department tends [editor: tends?] evaluates productivity on an annual basis, when the library prepares its statistics for the ARL Survey. As part of that survey, the department provides the numbers for borrowing and lending requests, as well as fill rate. Using ILLiad and OCLC statistics, the department head also prepares an evaluation of ILL statistics on annual reports prepared every January.

Although a formal mechanism to provide feedback is not in place, the ILL department pays careful attention to service- and productivity-related input provided by constituents through email, phone calls and in person. According to Battle, "Sometimes feedback can improve service, for example, when patrons asked for electronic delivery, Odyssey was implemented in 2004. Odyssey has improved service and saved staff time, printer wear and paper. We now deliver 90 percent of our articles in this manner."

"Tulane has a very high fill rate," says Battle, "because of excellent staff. The fill rate is 80 percent. Katrina hit the beginning of fiscal year 05-06, and we did not start lending until after that fiscal year, since mail was unreliable in New Orleans. We continued to borrow but were closed to January of 06. We are now borrowing and lending at the same level as before the storm."

Best Management Advice for Other Academic ILL Departments

"Certainly rely more on lending consortia," advises Battle, "to save mailing costs and to save other per item costs associated with borrowing. ILLiad, of course, streamlines the ILL process, makes it easier and cheaper, and has the robust ability to provide data and reports that you can use to evaluate services. My best advice for services is to listen to patrons and your employees, see what can be done to solve recurring problems, and try to provide the best service possible."

University of Minnesota

Cherie Weston, Head, Interlibrary Loan, University of Minnesota Libraries

I. Description of the University of Minnesota and Library

The University of Minnesota Libraries support the research, teaching and outreach mission of the University of Minnesota, a major public research university. The University has 40,572 undergraduate students; 25,527 graduate, professional and other students; and 4,088 full-time faculty. The University offers doctorates in more than 100 programs (including agriculture) and has several professional schools, including law, medicine, dentistry, veterinary medicine, nursing and business.

The University Libraries are located in five major facilities and eight branch libraries; the Law Library reports to the Law School and is administratively separate from the University Libraries. The University Libraries hold more than 6,800,000 physical volumes and have current subscriptions to more than 77,000 print and electronic journals. The University Libraries loan more materials than any other library in North America.

For FY 2007-2008, the University of Minnesota Libraries borrowed 34,465 items and loaned 29,785 items to other libraries. (Figures do not include the Bio-Med library, which lends materials through their own OCLC and DOCLINE® symbols, with a volume similar to MNU lending. The Libraries' collections are also heavily used by MINITEX, the state interlibrary loan agency, to supply materials to in-state libraries. MINITEX numbers are not included.)

II. Description of Staffing and ILL Budget

The University of Minnesota Libraries ILL staff is split between borrowing and lending, and includes the following: **MNU Borrowing** – [editor: bold OK?] Head, Library Manager; Library Assistant III (4); Library Assistant II (1); Student assistant (1); **MNU Lending** - Library Manager (1); Library Supervisor (1); Library Assistants (1.5) and students. Cherie Weston, Head, Interlibrary Loan (listed below under MNU Borrowing as "Head, Library Manager") supervises the borrowing unit. Lending is combined with MINITEX's Document Delivery Unit and is located in Andersen Library with a separate staff. Lending processes requests from out-of-state borrowing libraries. Document Delivery is one of 11 MINITEX programs. MINITEX is a unit of the University Libraries and supplies materials to in-state libraries.

MNU Borrowing:

Head, Library Manager: Responsible for overall management of unit, special project development and service enhancements.

Library Assistant III (4): Processes incoming requests (includes verification, finding suppliers, purchasing articles from document suppliers, selecting monographs for purchase), trains staff, runs statistical reports for collection development, works with systems staff on web maintenance, customizes and serves as expert user for ILLiad software, answers phone, email and service window questions.

Library Assistant II (1): Processes all incoming materials, (assigns due dates, notes restrictions), monitors Ariel workstations, requests replacement pages, returns material to lending library. Answers phone and service window questions.

Student Assistant (1 working 8-10 hours per week): Completes processing of returnables (affixes the book strips, routes materials, shelves the material at circulation, clears pickup shelves and sends email availability notices). Since these tasks only take one to two hours, borrowing began using circulation students for these duties during the fall semester of 2008. A big plus is that circulation handles all the hiring and payroll functions.

MNU Lending:

Library Manager, role (1): Monitors workflow, formulates operational procedures, identifies and analyzes operational problems and makes changes as appropriate to improve DTU request management. Serves as backup and resource for other DTU staff as needed.

Library Supervisor, role (1): Supervises and handles the day-to-day activities within the unit, including directing staff, handling request problems via phone and mail, compiling data and statistics on a monthly basis.

Library Assistants (1.5) and students: Handle the day-to-day work in the unit, which includes verification, retrieval of items, preparing items for shipment and processing returns. The ILL department has extended the hours that staff are available to process requests, which resulted in improved turnaround time for lending requests.

Staff Education

MNU Borrowing: The Libraries offer a suite of training classes that are available to all staff. "Staff have the opportunity to attend locally held conferences and may submit travel requests for ALA and other conferences," says Weston. "The University also offers management and training courses, and staff may also use Regents scholarships to enroll in academic courses at the University." The ILL head generally attends ALA Annual and Midwinter and the OCLC ILLiad conference.

MNU Lending: Staff in MNU lending have opportunities to attend workshops sponsored by the university on various HR topics. In addition, they may attend any MINITEX-sponsored conferences or training if interested, and the Library Manager and Library Supervisor attend the MINITEX ILL Conference each year. Often LM and LS staff also attend one or more days of the Minnesota Library Association meeting. "The Library Manager attended the Colorado ILL conference this past year," reports Weston. "Each staff member has, in addition, $200 to spend for conferences or classes."

Placement of ILL Department in Library's Organization

MNU Borrowing: All borrowing requests for patrons on the Minneapolis and St. Paul campus are processed under the MNU OCLC symbol using ILLiad software the department shares with the lending office. The borrowing office is part of the Information Access and Delivery Services Department of the Access Services Division and is located in Wilson Library. Staff from the Bio-Medical Library process the requests submitted by patrons affiliated with Health Sciences through a remote desktop application. Bio-Med uses a separate instance of ILLiad for their ILL lending operation.

MNU Lending: Lending is combined with MINITEX's Document Delivery Unit and is located in Andersen Library. Document Delivery is one of 11 MINITEX programs. MINITEX is a unit of the University Libraries.

Role in Collections and Acquisitions

MNU Borrowing: ILL head is a member of the Collections Council.

Budget Information

MNU Borrowing: 2008 expenditures for staff, fringe benefits, general operating supplies, IFM, article purchasing, printing, software, courier, postage, telephone, maintenance, administration, network costs and university assessments were $446,200.
The office also receives $15,000 in collection funds used to purchase monographs for the collection.

MNU Lending: 2008 revenues from invoices and IFM credits were $255,000. Expenditures for staff, fringe benefits, general operating supplies, printing, software, courier, postage, telephone, maintenance, administration, network costs and university assessments were $231,748.

Best Management Advice for Other Academic ILL Departments

MNU Borrowing: "When requesting articles that have reached the "Rule of Five," do check document suppliers and vendors since their price can be less expensive than requesting via ILL and then paying the royalty plus the lending fee," Weston suggests.

MNU Lending: "We don't have a typical lending situation since our requests are combined with MINITEX lending requests," reports Weston. "We have taken advantage of using the same staff to retrieve from campus libraries, which has been beneficial. Also, even though it can be difficult to implement new technology, it has almost always resulted in better service for the borrowing libraries, such as with implementing Odyssey."

III. Software and Automation

MNU Borrowing: "We use ILLiad to manage all of our interlibrary loan requests," Weston states. "ILLiad includes an interface with DOCLINE—the next upgrade is slated to improve this interface and will streamline the current process that involves inputting the request into DOCLINE and then screen-scraping the request."

MNU Lending: "We use OCLC's ILLiad to track all lending requests, regardless of how we receive them," relates Weston. "We do receive requests via email and our Web site, which are entered into ILLiad for handling, tracking and billing purposes."

Electronic Delivery

MNU Borrowing: All libraries that send via Odyssey are marked as Trusted Senders. This means that borrowing staff never need to handle any of the incoming documents as they are automatically posted to the Web and the patron is sent an e-mail notice of availability. The notice includes a statement asking the patron to notify us if the article needs to be replaced.

All articles that arrive via Ariel are exported to ILLiad and then delivered to the Web. Articles that arrive via U.S. mail are scanned upon arrival and delivered to the Web whenever possible. "We mail articles to the patron's preferred address if we are unable to scan the print copy," says Weston.

MNU Lending: "We send copy requests via Ariel or Odyssey whenever the borrowing institution has the ability to receive those documents," relates Weston. "We retrieve items for lending at 30 campus libraries and have a total of nine scanners. Six of our scanners are in the four major campus libraries: two scanners each in Wilson and Bio-Medical library, and one each in Walter and Magrath. We also have three scanners in the MINITEX office, which we use to transmit articles from those libraries without scanners."

Recent Software and Automation Enhancements

MNU Borrowing: "We merged the borrowing activity of our Bio-Medical library into the ILLiad software used by the Wilson borrowing office to streamline the interface we present to our patrons," Weston reports. "We also set up routing rules to automatically transfer the requests to the appropriate staff (the Bio-Med library requests the majority of their material via DOCLINE®)." All incoming material is handled by the Wilson office. Staff are able to offer assist each other if there are difficult citations and in cases of staffing shortages.

ILLiad introduced Web Circulation for ILL loans in early 2008. Web Circulation eliminated the need to have ILLiad clients installed at the six library pickup locations, resulting in fewer upgrades for systems staff.

MNU Lending: In Spring 2007 the department implemented Odyssey sending. In 2006, one of the employees developed an in-house program that allowed staff to automate the overdue/lost book process using ILLiad data that e-mails overdue notices to the borrowing institution.

Best Management Advice for Other Academic ILL Departments

MNU Borrowing: ILL management software allows staff to track all the activity involved in the ILL process. The system is available 24/7 for patrons to request materials. According to Weston, "The interface with WorldCat is great; you can easily customize the software. The interface to the Copyright Clearance Center saves an incredible amount of time."

MNU Lending: "ILLiad allows us to have all of our requests on one system, which makes it much easier to track everything," says Weston. "In addition, it allows us to have a single procedure for billing and sending overdue and lost book notifications."

IV. Resource Sharing Consortia

MNU Borrowing: "We are members of the CIC and RLG SHARES (see description below)," relates Weston. "Our statewide network, MINITEX, has its headquarters in one of our campus libraries. MINITEX manages our lending operation and also our remote storage, the Minnesota Library Access Center (MLAC), which is located in the subterranean level below their offices."

MNU Lending: MINITEX -- The lending division of the University of Minnesota shares an office and some staff with MINITEX Library Information Network, which is a statewide ILL service. There is overlap of staff, which handle both types of requests. MINITEX and MNU Lending requests are retrieved, copied and scanned using similar procedures.

✍ SHARES is an RLG collaboration that enables participating institutions to agree on prices, procedures and policies; monitor their own performance; and manage workflow to support increased lending activities. In addition, this program gives each participant's faculty, students and staff on-site access to collections and services at other SHARES institutions.

✍ CIC (Committee on Institutional Cooperation) is a consortium of 12 research universities, including the 11 members of the Big Ten Conference and the University of Chicago. The CIC Center for Library Initiatives fosters collaboration among research libraries to optimize student and faculty access to the combined resources of member libraries; maximize cost, time, and space savings for the libraries and their staffs; and support a collaborative environment where library staff can work together to solve their mutual problems.

MNU Borrowing: Membership in the CIC offers an array of library services. The CIC actively negotiates electronic licenses and cooperative purchases. ILL directors meet regularly at conferences and via conference calls to discuss resource sharing initiatives. Software vendors may be asked to join us to discuss enhancement requests. The CIC also contracts with a shipping firm to provide daily pickup and delivery of bins moving between institutions. Bins travel between eight states (Illinois, Indiana, Iowa, Michigan, Minnesota, Ohio, Pennsylvania and Wisconsin) according to a guaranteed delivery schedule. The CIC libraries do not charge each other for interlibrary loan.

Membership in the SHARES programs offers access to materials that would not circulate to nonmembers. Returnables are generally loaned for four weeks and renewals are allowed. Requests for rare and special collections materials are reviewed on a case-by-case basis. A minimal charge is assessed for transactions to offset labor and shipping costs.

The University of Minnesota Libraries is also a member of the Center for Research Libraries. Membership allows interlibrary loan access to their vast research collections.

In addition, consortia are frequently able to negotiate better pricing with commercial document delivery suppliers.

MNU Lending: "In the case of our lending department being merged with MINITEX Document Delivery, we are able to use the same staff to retrieve items at each individual campus library. We are staffed to retrieve and copy items from each library on a daily basis or multiple times a day in our largest libraries."

V. Commercial Document Delivery

MNU Borrowing: "We are purchasing an increasing number of articles, especially e-prints that are released ahead of publication," says Weston. "In many cases, it is faster and less expensive to purchase from a vendor than to request the item via ILL and then later pay the royalty fees on top of a lending fee. We look for purchase options whenever we cannot locate a holding library and as we work on unfilled requests. We do not differentiate based upon patron category but may query the patron about exceedingly expensive items. We use a purchasing card if the vendor doesn't bill us."

The University of Minnesota Libraries routinely purchases from NTIS, Harvard Business and SAE. They have accounts set up with the British Library's Inside service, BLDSC, CAI and CISTI as well as several vendors such as Elsevier, Ingenta, Meta Press. Royalties vary among document suppliers and vendors so they may look for the least expensive source.

ILL mediates all article requests because patrons do not always locate the library's licensed and locally owned materials. The Libraries do not impose any limits on the amount of material ordered by constituents. Document delivery fees are tracked as part of ILL expenses.

Fee-Based Services

The libraries do have fee-based services for external customers that are separate from interlibrary loan.

Best Management Advice for Other Academic ILL Departments

Weston offers the following advice for other libraries: "Do look for commercial suppliers. The price may end up being less expensive than paying an ILL lender and also paying copyright royalties."

VI. Copyright and Licensing

ILL Copyright-Compliant Policy or Guidelines

MNU Borrowing: The University of Minnesota Libraries apply Fair Use (Section 107). ILLiad tracks transactions that have exceeded the "Rule of Five"; all article requests include a copyright code that follows the CONTU Guidelines. The CIC consortium negotiated a discounted rate on the transactional reporting fee charged by the CCC. Royalty fees are paid on an annual basis to the Copyright Clearance Center. The department verifies the data and then uses the CCC interface within ILLiad to automatically export the transactions; an invoice arrives a short time later.

MNU Lending Statement: Before processing borrowing requests from other libraries, lending staff ensure that the library has provided a copyright compliance code.

Best Management Advice for Other Academic ILL Departments

Weston advises:

- ✍ Use an ILL management software that will track your data. Find one that will export the data to the CCC.
- ✍ Staff who negotiate licenses with vendors should, as a routine, request ILL lending provisions. They should also try to negotiate a reduced price for per-article purchasing from non-subscribed journals that the vendor also licenses. For instance, the ILL department has an account with a major vendor used to purchase individual articles. The set price is substantially less than the royalty charged by the CCC.

Electronic Licensing Agreements for Lending

The University of Minnesota Libraries boast ILL rights for 89 percent of their e-journals because their electronic resources librarian always asks.

Major ILL Copyright and Licensing Issues

MNU Lending: The need to keep abreast of provisions for ILL within the various licenses is a major issue for interlibrary loan lending. Lending still doesn't have a great tool for managing these resources and the rights that are included. Stipulations in delivery mechanisms, such as the requirement to use Ariel, hamper the library's use of other e-delivery tools. Having to print out a paper copy of the article and re-scan it takes staff time and is wasted paper. Weston would like to move toward sending the e-file directly to the borrowing library – or better yet, to the patron.

45

VII. Institutional Repositories and Open Access

Obtaining Materials from Open Access Journals or Institutional Repositories

The University of Minnesota Libraries use SFX to identify licensed resources. Patrons click a "Find It" icon found within enabled databases and indexes. If full-text is not available, they can initiate an ILL request. Systems staff also configured an automatic ISSN check of our OPAC to look for print holdings prior to creating the ILL request. Additionally, ILL staff perform a quick "Find It" search for full-text and print holdings. Staff also check the URLs found in OCLC bibliographic records for access to sample issues or other freely available material. Requests are cancelled as "available full-text" – the cancellation reason includes the library's licensed resources and also material freely available on the web.

The library's request volume has remained stable for the last three years. Staff are finding an increasing number of reports and nongovernment publications on the Web; some are freely available while others may be for sale.

VIII. Service Priorities for Constituents

The University of Minnesota Libraries provide free ILL services to all currently enrolled undergraduate and graduate students and to all current faculty and staff of the University of Minnesota – Twin Cities (TC) campus (Minneapolis and St. Paul). This includes services for patrons affiliated with our Academic Health Center. (All interlibrary loan borrowing transactions are requested under the OCLC symbol MNU although our Bio-Medical Library maintains a separate lending operation under the OCLC symbol UMM.) Patrons affiliated with programs located outside the metropolitan area -- such as Extension Services, the Hormel Institute (in Austin, MN), the Rochester campus and the Duluth Pharmacy and Medical School programs -- also receive services. Services are provided to distance education students. Services are also provided for emeritus faculty, retired staff and to visiting scholars officially affiliated with a campus department. Services for Law School affiliates are provided by the Law Library Interlibrary Loan office.

Services are basically the same for all eligible patron categories, although there are a few exceptions:

- Off-campus delivery: the department charges a small shipping fee for delivery to an off campus address. This option is available to all patrons.
- Returnables are not shipped to patrons who are physically located outside the continental U.S.
- Some patrons affiliated with the TC Medical and Pharmacy programs are located

on the Duluth campus of the University that is 150 miles north of the Twin Cities. These patrons request articles from the TC campus ILL service but request their loans through the Duluth ILL service.

Returnables: service is provided regardless of format.

- ✍ Interlibrary loan will attempt to borrow books, older bound periodicals, newspapers, microfilm, microfiche, scores, VHS, DVDs, CDs.
- ✍ Requests are accepted for items that are lost or missing from the collection.
- ✍ Requests are accepted for items that are in use (checked out) or at the bindery.
- ✍ ILL request items from abroad for material that is not available in the U.S.
- ✍ ILL staff will purchase English-language material published within the last five years or so if it is not available from preferred lenders (the CIC consortium), if it costs less than $150 and if it fits collection policies. ILL receives $15,000 each year from the collections budget for this project. ILL staff select material in Gobi (Yankee Book Peddler database used by Technical Services) for all of the campus library collections. Materials are RUSH-ordered and generally arrive within three to six days. If YBP does not have the item in stock, technical service staff will place the order with another supplier such as amazon.com. Orders are also placed for material that has not yet been published as long as there is a record in GOBI— these materials arrive shelf-ready. The interlibrary loan request is cancelled once the item has been selected and the patron is notified that the item is being purchased and told that they will be notified once it arrives.
- ✍ The Libraries DO NOT request required textbooks.
- ✍ ILL may cancel requests for popular materials found to be in constant demand.
- ✍ If materials are found to be available on campus, staff may initiate a paging request based upon the patron's preferences.

    [editor: should this be flush left?] Articles: All patrons receive the same services for articles. Staff will purchase articles if they are not available via ILL and, in many cases, once copyright has reached the CONTU "Rule of Five". This fee is not passed on to the patron.

ILL Services for Community Members, Visiting Scholars or Other Institutions

The Libraries do not offer services to community members or other institutions. ILL will offer services for visiting scholars if they are officially affiliated with a campus department and may make an occasional exception for special circumstances.

Special Services to Constituents

The department does not offer special ILL services but will do its best to rush materials when requested. The department will request replacement pages for the periodicals staff.

Notification and Delivery of Materials

ILLiad software sends an email as soon as the material is available.

- ✍ Articles: All articles are posted to the Web to a secure site for pickup (access) by the patron whenever possible; they are mailed to the patron's address if they cannot be delivered electronically. Some PDFs are sent via email.

- ✍ Returnables: Patrons select their preferred pickup location from six major campus libraries; faculty and staff can also select delivery to their campus office; all patrons can select delivery to their home address (a small fee is charged for postage).

IX. Services to Distance Learning Students

"We do not differentiate between on-campus and distance learning students," states Weston. "We make every effort to provide services regardless of where the patron may be located."

Document delivery of locally held material is available to all patron categories. "While we will not deliver interlibrary loan materials to patrons located outside the U.S., material owned by our library can be delivered to patrons who are living abroad. We lend locally held materials via interlibrary loan to foreign libraries so there isn't any reason to not do so for our own patrons," Weston explains.

X. Special Collections

Ten separate libraries within the University of Minnesota Libraries are primarily "special collections." Requests received by the ILL lending office are given to the appropriate person (or curator) at each library who will determine whether or not the item can be loaned or copied.

Requests come to interlibrary loan and the department works with the various libraries holding special collections. The type of material loaned varies and is determined at each individual library. If a rare item is loaned, the library specifies "in library use only." If the curator wished further supervision of the material, staff calls the borrowing library to ensure its ability to comply. ILL will ship things in boxes (not padded envelopes) that are fitted to the book for extra protection. Staff ship UPS so that items can be tracked if something becomes lost en route. ILL includes any special shipping instructions that the curator requires but normally does not include shipping instructions for the borrower. The onus is on the borrower to ship it back safely because they will pay for any damage to the book once it has left the lender's possession (this is in the national ILL code).

Digitization has little effect on what ILL is doing right now. Currently, most special collections items — unless they are duplicate microfilm — do not lend. ILL makes copies of materials that are in the public domain, when possible, and charges a base fee and a per-page fee when it gets too long. Curators do not seem to be digitizing materials instead of copying or lending.

The University of Minnesota Libraries follow the ACRL *Guidelines for the Interlibrary Loan of Rare and Unique Materials* (revised June 2004). Interlibrary Loan does not assess additional fees for these materials beyond our normal fee structure.

XI. Measuring Productivity and Evaluating Services

Borrowing: "We use the Web reports feature of ILLiad and also run more detailed Access reports as necessary for collection development," Weston relates. "We use OCLC reports, including special consortial reports for data on CIC and RLG SHARES. Reports are run on a monthly basis and as needed to gather data to analyze work processes."

ILLiad has a report that shows the average time between each stage of an ILL transaction submitted by patron, first handled by ILL staff, request sent, request received, patron notified). This report is used to look at the stages when the request is within the department's control and to determine if there is a way to reduce the time that each process takes. For instance, ILL reduced article turnaround time by increasing the number of times that staff check the Ariel workstation throughout the day.

Turnaround time reports can be run in ILLiad based on various categories of suppliers (such as CIC, RLG SHARES, DOCLINE, document supplier). Staff adjust the custom holdings groups based on this data.

Lending: "We gather data from OCLC and ILLiad to prepare a monthly statistical report that includes data on number of copies and loans, IFM credits, invoice amount and turnaround time," Weston reports. "Specifically we use the OCLC Usage Statistics: the ILL Fee Management Program Lender Report and the Lender Activity Overview Report. We also use the ILLiad Reports/Lending Reports: Fill-Rate Statistics. From there, we can generate reports with information about various constituent groups so that we have a better idea of where things are going."

Other Tools Used to Evaluate Productivity and Service
Borrowing: ILL looks at LibQual data and has conducted short customer service surveys.

After looking at ways to reduce turnaround time for articles, ILL began using the Trusted

Sender feature in ILLiad (all suppliers that use ILLiad's Odyssey software to scan articles are marked as Trusted Sender). Articles are automatically posted to the Web whenever they are supplied by a lender that uses Odyssey. Staff adjusted the custom holdings to include Odyssey users as a preferred supplier category. Because articles that arrive by this method are not reviewed by staff, the arrival notice instructs the patron to contact ILL if there are any problems with the article. In addition to improving turnaround time and the ergonomic benefit, the feature freed up several hours of staff time for other duties.

Lending: Once a year, staff track turnaround time and measure how much time requests take in each step of the lending process. "We do this by selecting a sample – usually 100 requests per day for one work week (these are from a variety of sources, and include MINITEX and MNU requests.)," explains Weston. "Staff record date and time that the request moved from one process to the next for verification, retrieval, copying and sending. We have concentrated on specific areas of request processing when looking at these measurements. We constantly monitor our turnaround time and evaluate staffing based on the numbers. Last year, we added evening staffing to ensure that there were additional downloads from ILLiad, resulting in faster service."

Indiana University-Purdue University Indianapolis (IUPUI)

Tina Baich, Visiting Assistant Librarian, Interlibrary Services/Bibliographic and Metadata Services Team, IUPUI University Library

I. Description of IUPUI and Library

Indiana University-Purdue University Indianapolis (IUPUI), a partnership between Indiana and Purdue Universities, is Indiana's urban research and academic health sciences campus. IUPUI's mission is to advance the state of Indiana and the intellectual growth of its citizens to the highest levels nationally and internationally through research and creative activity, teaching and learning, and civic engagement. By offering a distinctive range of bachelor's, master's, professional and doctoral degrees, IUPUI promotes the educational, cultural and economic development of central Indiana and beyond through innovative collaborations, external partnerships and a strong commitment to diversity.

The IUPUI University Library honors tradition but looks to the innovative application of technology and new forms of engagement with our various publics as our path to excellence. Current holdings within the libraries at IUPUI include over 1,338,889 volumes, more than 36,000 current periodicals and journals, over 1,197,000 microforms, and more than 152,400 government documents and audiovisual materials. Services are available to university students, faculty and staff, as well as individual citizens, businesses, professional firms, and public agencies. Wisdom demands the sharing of knowledge. We, therefore, collect, organize and assist in the use of the record of human understanding. We preserve the records of the past; we help individuals inform themselves in the present, and we shape the information environment for the future.

During the 2007-2008 fiscal year, the University Library's Interlibrary Services Department borrowed 17,997 items and loaned 36,942. The department also filled an additional 2,257 document delivery requests from its own collection. The total number of requests filled was 57,196.

II. Description of Staffing and ILL Budget

The Interlibrary Services Department consists of an Interlibrary Loan Librarian, one Interlibrary Services Senior Assistant, an Interlibrary Loan Clerk, and two to three Interlibrary Services Student Assistants. Tina Baich is the Interlibrary Loan Librarian.

ILL Librarian (1):

- ✍ Supervises ILS team to ensure all ILS requests are being processed in a timely manner.
- ✍ Helps with ILS requests during times of heavy volume or to locate hard-to-find items.
- ✍ Assists patrons with their requests and usage of library resources.
- ✍ Monitors financial expenditures and income.
- ✍ Maintains and monitors reciprocal agreements.
- ✍ Communicates with lending and borrowing libraries.
- ✍ Maintains Web pages for interlibrary services.
- ✍ Supports team leader for access services team with other duties and projects as assigned.

Interlibrary Services Senior Assistant (1):

- ✍ Oversees the daily operation of interlibrary borrowing, request delivery, Rapid and document delivery services.
- ✍ Acts as a backup for interlibrary lending operations.
- ✍ Acts as liaison with the interlibrary and request delivery operations of the other I.U. libraries and with interlibrary operations around and outside the state.
- ✍ Hires, trains and supervises student workers.

Interlibrary Loan Clerk (1)

- ✍ Oversees the processing of lending materials from our collections to other libraries.
- ✍ Acts as a backup for interlibrary borrowing operations.
- ✍ Assists with the hiring, training and supervision of student workers.

Interlibrary Services Student Assistants (2.5-3 FTE)

- ✍ Pull materials from library stacks.
- ✍ Process mail.
- ✍ Process outgoing and incoming materials.
- ✍ Scan articles for electronic delivery.

Staff Education

Library staff are provided with professional development funds that can be used to attend workshops, conferences or other events as deemed appropriate. IUPUI's Human Resources Administration also offers a number of workshops free of charge to staff. The ILL Librarian encourages staff to take advantage of opportunities she feels would be especially helpful to their work.

Placement of ILL Department in Library's Organization

Interlibrary services falls under the access services team, which also includes circulation, reserves, stacks management and security. "The size of our staff does not allow for a departmental split between borrowing and lending," Baich reports. "Of our two full-time staff members, however, one has overall responsibility for lending while the other is responsible for borrowing."

Role in Collections and Acquisitions

Interlibrary services implemented a "Purchase on Demand" program in 2005 that allows the staff to forward qualified items to Acquisitions for purchase. The goals of this program include:

- ? Allowing the IUPUI University Library to quickly provide patrons access to recent titles that are difficult or impossible to borrow.
- ? Add titles in interdisciplinary fields or emerging topics that may be missed/unfunded through traditional collection development activities.
- ? Achieve the dual goals of meeting immediate needs and adding potentially high-use titles to the collection.

The library has found that the titles purchased through this program have a higher rate of circulation and most frequently fill the needs of faculty and graduate students. Staff will purchase titles published in the current year or the preceding three, that do not exceed one hundred dollars. Paperback format is preferred, and fiction is allowed. Staff follow other criteria, and will not purchase titles available from the Indiana University Library system, or other titles the library normally would not collect.

The ILL Librarian does work with subject librarians to provide journal information to assist them in collection development decisions. A number of reports were recently mounted on the library intranet for subject librarians to easily access ILL statistics.

Budget Information

Major spending categories are wages, shipping costs, copyright, subscription/license fees for OCLC, ILLiad and RapidILL, and borrowing fees (IFM and invoices). Our borrowing fees are offset by the lending fees we charge. An overall budget figure was not available, but staff salaries alone are approximately $93,000.00.

Best Management Advice for Other Academic ILL Departments

"Always look for ways to minimize costs," advises Baich. "For instance, is it cheaper to buy an article directly from the publisher than to pay a borrowing fee and copyright? Can you better structure your custom holdings to borrow from free lenders more frequently? Can you request reciprocal agreements with libraries you frequently borrow from that aren't free now?"

III. Software and Automation

Our primary resource sharing software is ILLiad, but we also use RapidILL. "We became a Rapid library in the fall of 2007 and love the service," Baich says. "Once Rapid lending is integrated with ILLiad, our workflow will be far improved. Using Rapid to search against our journal holdings has already streamlined our ILLiad processing."

Electronic Delivery

The Interlibrary Services Department primarily uses Odyssey, but still uses Ariel because there are those that do not have Odyssey. However, even articles received in Ariel are imported into ILLiad for processing to the patron. Borrowing articles are stored on the ILLiad server and "delivered" to the patron's ILLiad account.

Recent Software and Automation Enhancements

"With the new version of ILLiad (7.3), a couple of new services became available," notes Baich, "Web Circulation and Odyssey Helper. Both have helped streamline our workflow. Web Circulation lets our circulation staff check out ILL items at the desk. Odyssey Helper enables staff to utilize scanners to process documents electronically within ILLiad for both document delivery and lending requests. These time-savers allow staff to focus on other tasks."

Best Management Advice for Other Academic ILL Departments

"I wish all libraries would implement Odyssey either as part of ILLiad or the stand-alone version," says Baich. "It is very easy to use and greatly reduces staff-mediation of requests. Achieving the highest level of unmediated processing possible is a huge part of improving service as volume grows. Take the time to look at all your workflows and statistics to find ways to capture efficiencies."

IV. Resource Sharing Consortia

"As part of the Indiana University Libraries system, we participate in a remote circulation service called Request Delivery," Baich reports. "Patrons are able to order materials from other campuses through the shared OPAC, IUCAT. We also participate in reciprocal lending with other Indiana libraries. The *Indiana Library Resource Sharing Manual* encourages reciprocal borrowing among Indiana libraries, and the majority of Indiana libraries have agreed to follow this policy. In addition, Indiana also has a statewide courier that minimizes shipping expenses."

"We are also a member of RapidILL, a service that provides 24-hour turnaround time of articles free of charge to participating libraries. Approximately two-thirds of our article borrowing requests were filled through RapidILL during the 2007-2008 academic year. This averages out to a base fee of only $1.50, give or take, for each transaction. This is much more cost effective than borrowing for a fee from other sources. The fast turnaround time is a huge plus from the patron's perspective. Since we have joined RapidILL, we have been using document suppliers less. Paying copyright alone is often more affordable than purchasing an article from a document supplier."

V. Commercial Document Delivery

The IUPUI University library relies on document providers for lower costs, preprints and difficult to borrow items. Commonly used suppliers include Ingenta, Sage, the British Library, and Harvard Business Publishing. "However, we often go directly to the source of the journal if they offer pay-per-article service," says Baich.

"I typically compare the cost of the document supplier to that of the borrowing/copyright cost before going with a document supplier. If articles are not available directly from a publisher or Ingenta, I turn to the British Library to provide articles. The department does not have a formal method in place for tracking document delivery service fees, but based on transaction-by-transaction comparisons I believe we save money and time when we choose to go through a document supplier."

Unmediated or Mediated Access to Document Delivery Services

"We do not have any open accounts where users can order articles and the library is charged," says Baich. "There is some concern that users would be confused about when they would be charged. With the turnaround times we have been able to achieve, it seems simpler to have users submit all requests to ILL and we will make the purchase if that is necessary."

Fee-Based Services

"We do charge lending fees for our materials, but I don't consider it to be competition with commercial suppliers," Baich says. "We simply charge in an attempt to cover some of the costs of lending. We have a maximum cost of $26 set for borrowing from other libraries."

VI. Copyright and Licensing

ILL Copyright-Compliant Policy or Guidelines

The Interlibrary Services Department observes the CONTU "Rule of Five," which is an inherent part of the ILLiad system. Once a journal appears on the copyright list in ILLiad, staff can decide whether to pay that copyright fee or go to a document provider. The department submits its copyright report to the CCC through ILLiad. CCC then bills the department for the amount owed.

Best Management Advice for Other Academic ILL Departments

"It is sometimes more cost effective to purchase an article directly from the publisher or another document supplier than to borrow as usual and pay copyright fees. Compare the costs before doing either. For larger operations, it may be helpful to pay copyright more frequently than on an annual basis," advises Baich.

Major ILL Copyright and Licensing Issues

According to Baich, "As more journals are available electronically, it is important to have ILL permissions included in license agreements and to have some way of managing those licenses so the information is readily available to ILL staff. Copyright fees continue to increase in some subject areas, which makes ILL copyright budgets tighter. There has been recent discussion of developing an Electronic Resources Management System to track licensing restrictions and other information. The ILL Librarian will be involved when this project gets underway."

VII. Institutional Repositories and Open Access

Obtaining Materials from Open Access Journals or Institutional Repositories

"We are part of the Open Access Pod in RapidILL, which provides us with access to these articles without having to search. I believe this Pod searches against the Directory of Open Access Journals to find materials," says Baich.

"Generally speaking, if an OCLC record makes note of something being open access, the staff search for it before ordering. We search all thesis/dissertation requests in Google Scholar before ordering in case electronic copies are available in institutional repositories. We search for all conference papers in Google, All Academic (www.allacademic.com), and sponsoring institution Web sites before pursuing other methods." Baich explains. "Our e-journal finder also includes a number of open access journals so we frequently find items that way."

"While more materials are readily available free of charge on the Internet, there is also a lot more material," maintains Baich. "We have found that many patrons have difficulty navigating the complex architecture of online resources. Therefore, we have not seen a decrease but rather an increase in requests even if the material is readily available online. We locate these materials for our patrons and alert them to its existence. The cost of processing these requests is, of course, less since there is no borrowing fee, but it still impacts staff and time costs."

VIII. Service Priorities for Constituents

The IUPUI University Library lending policy does not differentiate based on the status of the borrowing library's patron. Lending policies, including fess and loan periods, are as follows:
- Indiana libraries: no charge.
- Libraries with whom we have a reciprocal agreement: no charge.
- Nonprofit libraries: $15 OCLC IFM or $20 invoice per request.
- For-profit libraries: $20 OCLC IFM or $25 invoice per request.
- Rush requests and/or photocopies greater than 50 pages: $5 extra
- Circulation/renewal policy:
  Continental U.S.: 20 days for books, Alaska, Hawaii, Canada, International: 90 days for books, one week patron use for A/V materials (both U.S./International). Two renewal requests allowed. Items may be recalled if requested by an IUPUI constituent.

The only borrowing differentiation made among different patron categories is the request limit policy.

- ✍ Faculty: 400 items.
- ✍ Graduate students and staff: 125 items.
- ✍ Undergraduate students: 50 items.

There is no cost to our patrons to borrow materials. Electronic delivery of articles is the default, and patrons will only receive hard copies if scanning is not possible. The department will not accept requests for textbooks on the campus bookstore's textbook list.

ILL Services for Community Members, Visiting Scholars or Other Institutions

Through a partnership with Martin University, another Indianapolis educational institution, IUPUI University Library provides its students with interlibrary loan services. Community members are referred to their local public library to place ILL requests. Affiliates of other area educational institutions are able to place requests with their institutions.

The library does issue borrower cards to Indiana Residents and participate in the Academic Libraries of Indiana (ALI) Onsite Reciprocal Borrowing Program. This program allows students, faculty and staff from participating ALI libraries to borrow books from any other participating ALI library directly without using interlibrary loan.

Special Services to Constituents

As part of the Indiana University system, the library participates in Request Delivery, a remote circulation system that allows IU-affiliates to order items from other IU campuses through the OPAC. The Interlibrary Services Department is responsible for administering that service for IUPUI University library.

The department also created a Faculty Proxy service that allows faculty to have proxy accounts created for graduate and/or teaching assistants to request on their behalf.

"In Fall 2007, we piloted an Article Delivery Service, which allows patrons to place requests for articles available in journals held in our print collections," Baich reports. "This fall we are beginning to promote this service, which is open to all University Library affiliates."

If ILL staff are unable to locate an item based on the information provided by the patron, a staff member will send the patron an email requesting more information. This frequently results in an electronic dialogue between staff and patron that could be likened to a reference interview.

Notification and Delivery of Materials

All notifications are sent via e-mail. University Library handles interlibrary loan for the Herron Art Library as well so patrons have the option of picking up materials at either library. Articles are delivered electronically to the patron's ILLiad account whenever possible. If electronic delivery is not possible, the patron can choose between picking the article up at either library or having it mailed to them.

IX. Services to Distance Learning Students

IUPUI has seen an increase in the number of distance education students, which has caused a corresponding increase in ILL requests from these students.

"We recently created a custom queue in ILLiad to which distance education requests are automatically routed," says Baich. "This serves as a trigger to staff to follow the different procedures in place for distance education requests. For instance, we do not cancel requests from distant students if they are available at another campus library. We order the article for them since they are unable to come to campus."

Distance education students have always been able to request articles held in University Library collections, which are delivered to them electronically. The department, unfortunately, is only able to fill nonreturnable requests for distance education students at this time. Some distance education students live near other IU campuses. In these cases, the department is able to have returnables held within the IU system sent to their local campuses for pickup. For items not held in the IU system, interlibrary services currently refers distance education students to their local public libraries to place ILL requests.

There are currently 219 self-identified distance students registered with interlibrary services. An additional five distance faculty are registered. "This is a relatively small number in relation to total distance education enrollment. I believe this is due to the fact that many resources are available electronically and can be accessed by students off-campus without the need for interlibrary loan," says Baich.

X. Special Collections

"We do not generally loan materials from our special collections and archives. Should we receive a request for such material, we consult with the special collections staff," explains Baich. "They have final say on whether or not to lend. In consultation with our special collections staff, we are able to provide copy services for special collections materials within copyright guidelines."

"Our library has a large digitization program, which, I believe, has allowed many people to access information online rather than placing requests for original material. Special collections, in conjunction with our Digital Libraries Team, have mounted a number of online collections (http://www.ulib.iupui.edu/collections/digital/)," Baich maintains.

"Though we are rarely able to borrow special collections material from other libraries, we are always willing to accept any conditions of use they place on the materials as discussed in the guidelines. Although we are generally unable to loan our own special collections material, if no other lender is available we will query our special collections staff to see if a loan is possible," adds Baich.

XI. Measuring Productivity and Evaluating Services

The ILL Librarian runs annual reports on ILL productivity as well as any interim reports deemed necessary. ILLiad offers reports that provide most of the information the department finds valuable, such as number of requests finished, requests cancelled, requests by academic department and status, fill rate, turnaround time and most requested journals and books. "There are also reports that allow us to monitor requests outstanding for x number of days, copyright payments and who we borrow from/lend to most frequently," Baich explains.

The Interlibrary Services Department requests feedback from patrons, typically in the form of surveys, when implementing new services. The library as a whole engages in a yearly user survey. Plans are currently in the works for the library to conduct a LibQual survey this fall.

The department uses the statistics and survey responses to modify and enhance services. ILLiad statistics are used as a benchmark. "The department's goal is to surpass the previous year's productivity, and we have succeeded in this goal since I became the ILL Librarian two years ago. Such achievements promote morale and, therefore, staff productivity," Baich states.

Brigham Young University

Kathy Hansen, Access Services Department Chair, Harold B. Lee Library

I. Description of BYU and Library

Brigham Young University, established in 1875, is located 50 miles south of Salt Lake City in Provo UT. The university provides an outstanding education in an atmosphere consistent with the ideals and principles of its sponsor, The Church of Jesus Christ of Latter-day Saints.

Nearly 33,000 students were enrolled in BYU during 2008 representing all 50 states, the District of Columbia and more than 115 countries. BYU offers courses in 11 colleges, in Continuing Education and Graduate Studies, and in three general undergraduate areas of study. Many academic and professional programs are augmented by internships and career-related summer jobs. For fall semester 2008, bachelor's degrees were offered in 187 academic programs, master's degrees in 64, doctorates in 25 and juris doctorates in one. In the 2006-2007 academic school year, BYU awarded 8,130 undergraduate and graduate degrees. BYU fulltime employees include approximately 1,300 instructional faculty, 88.4 percent of whom are tenured or on tenure track, and approximately 2,900 administrative and staff personnel.

The Harold B. Lee Library provides many services, collections and computers for more than 15,000 students every day. The library contains over 8 million items including 3.3 million books, 27,000 journal titles, thousands of full-text databases and indexes, 250,000 maps, 3 million microfilms and more than 1 million photographs and prints. The library is located in the center of the BYU campus, features collections and services on six floors and occupies a footprint the equivalent of 2½ football fields from north to south. The library provides study seating for nearly 5,000 patrons including 800 public use computer stations. Approximately 77 FTE librarians, 40 FTE administrative staff, 40 FTE fulltime staff, 14.5 FTE part-time staff, and 400 student workers are employed by the library.

The Harold B. Lee Library borrowed 30,053 items and loaned 47,031 items to other libraries in 2008.

II. Description of Staffing and ILL Budget

The following staff comprise the ILL Department: a Document Delivery Manager, Interlibrary Loan Borrowing Supervisor, Interlibrary Loan Lending Supervisor, Digital Document Delivery Supervisor, Faculty and Graduate Document Delivery Supervisor, Copy Center Supervisors, and 12.5 student workers. Kathy Hansen, the Access Services Chair, is responsible for the overall supervision of the department.

- Document Delivery Manager: supervises the below listed supervisors; manages and directs the staff and workflow of the unit and assists with "special case" requests from each area.

- Interlibrary Loan Borrowing Supervisor: 3 FTE students; works with local patrons to borrow materials from other libraries.

- Interlibrary Loan Lending Supervisor: 4 FTE students; works with other libraries to retrieve in-house materials and deliver.

- Digital Document Delivery Supervisor: 1 FTE students; supervises the two Copy Center supervisors and assists with digital delivery processes.

- Faculty and Graduate Document Delivery Supervisor: 2.5 FTE students; works with local faculty and graduate patrons to retrieve materials and deliver.

- Copy Center Supervisors (2 20-hour employees): 2 FTE students; scans and photocopies requested materials.

Staff Education

The Document Delivery Manager is required to have a MLS and/or extensive library service to qualify for the position. We have procedure and training manuals for each of the ILL related areas.

The manager and the staff level employees have the opportunity to attend Bibliographic Center for Research (BCR is BYU's OCLC Regional Service Provider) training meetings held in state and may attend the Colorado and/or the Northwest ILL yearly conferences. A staff member (usually the Manager) attends GWLA (Greater Western Library Alliance) Resource Sharing conferences and OCLC/ILLiad meetings. The Manager attends ALA conferences and Utah Library Association annual conferences. The Manager may receive permission to travel for other consortia meetings. Travel costs are paid by the library.

All staff are encouraged to take advantage of campus technology and Human Resources classes and workshops. The Library frequently provides Web-based seminars from a variety of sources. All full-time staff have a full tuition benefit, which allows them to take university classes. The Library strongly encourages obtaining bachelors and advanced degrees using this benefit.

The Library provides partial tuition benefits for library staff (full-time and part-time employees) who want to obtain an MLS through distance education programs. At present, five of our ILL staff members are working on distance MLS degrees.

Placement of ILL Department in Library's Organization

The ILL Department is part of the Access Services Department which reports to the Public Services Division. Access Services also includes circulation, course reserve, media services and stacks management. ILL will eventually be responsible for auxiliary storage services.

Role in Collections and Acquisitions

ILL provides CCG reports for collection development listing how many times a periodical title has been requested. A collection development policy was created several years ago, which allows ILL Borrowing to purchase books requested by faculty patrons if the item is available in print and is not available for loan from another library. The Music Library purchases all music scores that are ordered via ILL and will soon start to purchase any CD or media titles requested via ILL.

"In the past 18 months, we began to order media items requested by faculty," Hansen reports. "We only purchase print and media items for faculty if they are not available from a lending institution or if they can be purchased less expensively than they can be borrowed (within approximately $30 - $50 cost range). These items are nearly always added to the collection. We also order items requested two or more times via ILL Borrowing. We consult subject specialists for approval if the item is being requested by nonfaculty patrons."

Budget Information

"We do have a set budget for student wages and for supplies," Hansen reports. "ILL income is also held in a budget that is used to pay for supplies and equipment for ILL and the larger access services department. The library allows ILL to use income funds to pay for equipment, supplies, maintenance costs, etc. We rely heavily on student employees throughout the university and the library."

Major Budget categories:

✍ Borrowing invoices

✍ Commercial vendor costs – British Library, etc.
✍ Maintenance fees
✍ Staffing
✍ Supplies
✍ Shipping
✍ Automation – ILLiad
✍ RapidILL
✍ OCLC costs
✍ Offsets: OCLC reimbursement, SHAREs reimbursement, UALC reimbursements

Approximate ILL Costs for Lee Library Interlibrary Loan for 2007

✍ $46,290.00 Borrowing and Lending costs
✍ $16,250.00 Ongoing costs for Ariel, ILLiad, RapidILL
✍ $145,935.00 Student wages (10.43 FTE)
✍ $190,790.00 Staff salaries (5.63 FTE)
✍ $26,165.00 Supplies, equipment
✍ $425,430.00 Total Costs
✍ $33,657.00 Income earned

Best Management Advice for Other Academic ILL Departments

"We are extremely fortunate to have a very supportive library administration," says Hansen. "We are well staffed; our student workers and staff members are well trained and dedicated to our service goals. All student raises are based on merit and we do student evaluations once a semester. The library administration has let us use our ILL income account to purchase needed equipment which is regularly upgraded; this allows us to provide excellent scanning services."

"Because Brigham Young University is supported by the Church of Jesus Christ of Latter-day Saints, our shipping costs are lower that usual because we are included in the Church's contract with FedEx," adds Hansen.

III. Software and Automation

"ILLiad is the basis for all of our ILL functions," reports Hansen. We try to use all features available to us in OCLC. We also use Rapid, DOCLINE, ALA and email."

Electronic Delivery and Software Enhancements

The department uses Ariel and Odyssey to scan all article requests and deliver them electronically. The department recently updated to ILLiad 7.3, so far the staff have not noticed any improvements or changes.

Best Management Advice for Other Academic ILL Departments

"Our patrons are especially happy with the ILL and Faculty Delivery 'buttons' that display in the item records in the library catalog and many of the serial databases," Hansen says. "Getting complete citation information has streamlined the ILL Borrowing and Faculty/Graduated Document Delivery services."

IV. Resource Sharing Consortia

The ILL department uses RapidILL, GWLA, DOCLINE, SHARES, BCR, CCLA (Church Consortium Library and Archives), and UALC (Utah Academic Library Consortium). The Harold B. Lee Library also participates in a number of reciprocal agreements with other libraries.

"About half of our requests are free because we fill them using consortium services," says Hansen. "Most consortia provide materials quickly and use good quality scans. RapidILL has made an enormous difference in our turnaround time and the satisfaction of our patrons with our services. They also help with unusual requests such as loans of runs of periodicals or even a set of comic books from a special collection (GWLA library)."

"We only use commercial document delivery services as a last option. We will always use our consortial partners first because of free reciprocal services," states Hansen.

"RapidILL has had enormous impact on our ILL Borrowing" adds Hansen. "We saw a significant drop in our turnaround times and a rise in user satisfaction with the articles we receive from RapidILL."

"Our membership in GWLA has been very beneficial to ILL and to our library," continues Hansen. "The GWLA pursuit of "ILL Best Practices" focus on ensuring that members provide accuracy, speed of delivery, and accessibility of materials to patrons. GWLA has set measurable conceptual, structural and procedural goals, which all member libraries strive to attain. GWLA has set quantifiable measures to assess if member libraries meet these goals and regularly assesses the ability of the libraries to meet these commitments."

V. Commercial Document Delivery

The department uses vendors when staff order the sixth article in the past five years of a title's publication (CCG). Commercial document delivery providers are uses them for preprints, and are also used when it might be faster.

"We use CISTI, British Library, National Library of Medicine," explains Hansen. "We don't use vendors unless we have to; we find it less expensive to conduct a second search for lending libraries with lower costs. We belong to many consortia, which results in loans for no cost. Our library has licensed many full-text databases, such as the recent Elsevier database which provides access to all their publications."

"We always use the least expensive source we can find," Hansen adds. "The Library is very supportive of ILL activity; our invoices are paid from a collection development budget."

Unmediated or Mediated Access to Document Delivery Services

"Our borrowing costs have been low enough that the library has not opted to initiate unmediated requests for materials from commercial vendors," Hansen says. "We do not impose borrowing limits upon our patrons in general; we might impose limits on a case by case basis."

Fee-Based Services

The Harold B. Lee Library charges $12.00 per article if the library does not have a reciprocal or consortial agreement with the borrowing library.

"We borrow from other libraries or consortia whenever we can," maintains Hansen. "We use commercial vendors when necessary for copyright purposes or when they are the last resort."

Best Management Advice for Other Academic ILL Departments

"Try to balance cost for service with turnaround time," Hansen advises. "We try to find a lender with lowest cost and quick service. We have been successful with this approach."

VI. Copyright and Licensing

ILL Copyright-Compliant Policy or Guidelines

The department uses the CONTU "Rule of Five" guidelines. The ILL department works closely with the campus copyright office. Staff use ILLiad to track copyright and to produce reports.

Best Management Advice for Other Academic ILL Departments

"Take full advantage of the Copyright Guidelines' 'Rule of Five'," suggests Hansen. "We go to commercial vendors when we order the sixth article to be sure we pay the necessary permission's fees. If needed, the department makes direct payments to publishers usually through invoicing or with vendors through a deposit account."

"We also use ILLiad to track our copyright statistics and share this information with subject selectors in the library. This information is used when purchasing new print titles and when the library is considering the purchase of serial databases."

Major ILL Copyright and Licensing Issues

"We have convinced library administration that ILL lending permission is crucial to receiving good ILL borrowing services," says Hansen. The Library has also responded to initiatives developed by the GWLA Resource Sharing Committee and the Utah College Library Council Resource Sharing Committee for negotiating license agreements and other shared resources. The GWLA has published "Guidelines for Licensing Electronic Resources" to help GWLA members negotiate contracts with vendors.

Copyright issues are lessened to a great extent because of licensing contracts for periodical titles in serial databases. The library vigorously pursues ILL lending clauses in its licensing agreements to include permission to use electronic items for ILL delivery. The librarian who manages licensing has also created a database that allows the ILL staff to check by periodical title to see if ILL has licensed copyright permissions to use full-text materials from the database.

According to Hansen, now that some vendors are making full runs of periodicals available, copyright concerns may lessen even more. "Our library and many others are aggressively pursuing digital collections," Hansen states. "The Library works closely with the campus Copyright Office to stay current with developments in copyright and when developing library policies."

VII. Institutional Repositories and Open Access

The department has not noticed any significant changes due to institutional repositories or open access journals. Workloads have increased steadily every year. Staff do not always search institutional repositories or other sources to locate materials, especially when they are busy.

"We have seen an increase in requests for theses and most of those are filled electronically from the granting institutions (presumably from their library or institutional repository)," reports Hansen. "BYU has digitized Mormon subject theses retroactively to 1930. Other theses have been digitized beginning in 2002 (although some grad students do not opt to provide digital copies). An analysis made of on-campus and off-campus hits to individual thesis titles show that some of the digital theses have been viewed more than 20,000 times. The Lee Library has been actively engaged in promoting institutional repository initiatives here at BYU for approximately six years. The university has become more actively involved in the issues in the past four or five years."

VIII. Service Priorities for Constituents

ILL and document delivery services are provided for free to BYU constituents. The department will not borrow course assigned textbooks for students, or borrow materials from international libraries for undergraduates.

ILL Services for Community Members, Visiting Scholars or Other Institutions

"We do a limited amount of borrowing for these types of patrons on a case-by-case basis," says Hansen. "We have set up some special arrangements for a few businesses -- mostly herbal remedy companies. We charge them a flat per request rate and bill them per month."

Special Services to Constituents

The ILL department offers document delivery service for faculty and graduate students, which allows them to request library-held materials. The staff retrieves the material, checks out, scans or photocopies the item. Faculty materials are delivered to their offices; graduate materials are made available in the ILL office for pickup. Ariel is used for electronic delivery of scanned materials. Staff also renew or pick up returning circulating materials for faculty. The ILL office processed 21,420 requests (20,570 filled) for the faculty document delivery service in 2008.

Nearly all of the borrowing requests come in through ILLiad (remote user). If the patron comes into the office and requests assistance, department staff will help them. This help may include a reference interview.

"Occasionally we get requests for enhanced services from our faculty, such as a request made by a faculty member who wanted to receive all his article materials in full text," says Hansen. "Essentially he wanted us to convert his scanned requests to text files for him. We researched the possibility of providing this level of service and it can be done. But we are not currently staffed to support this type of service for all of our patrons – however, developments in technology may permit this type of service to become routine in the near future."

Notification and Delivery of Materials

"We notify our student and community patrons via ILLiad generated email that loaned materials are available," Hansen explains. "We use ILLiad generated email to notify all patrons that scanned materials are available and include a link to the article in the email. In addition to ILLiad email messages, all faculty patrons will have their loaned materials (books or articles that arrive in print) delivered to their department office. We will provide print copies of Ariel documents if a faculty member specifically requests a print copy. All other patrons must pick up loaned print materials in the ILL office."

IX. Services to Distance Learning Students

ILL Borrowing only accepts requests for monographic materials available from the Howard B. Lee Library from distance education or continuing education patrons. Staff members mail circulating items to the patron if they live far enough away that coming to campus would be prohibitive, or if the patron has special circumstances such as a disability. Article requests for distance learning are treated the same as the faculty and graduate delivery requests – items are retrieved, checked out or scanned or photocopies. Patrons are notified that scanned/photocopied items are available in ILLiad via an email notice.

If monographic materials are unavailable from BYU, staff will refer them to their local library's interlibrary loan.

"We have noticed an increase of requests for distance learning students this year; however, the number of requests from distance learning patrons is low," states Hansen. "We have been told that one of the requirements for the instructors who put the distance education courses together, is that they must provide the student with all the necessary reading materials needed to complete the course."

"We don't charge distance education students or any campus related patron for ILL or Faculty/Graduate Document Delivery services," adds Hansen.

X. Special Collections

With the permission of the special collections staff, we will scan articles or chapters to provide digital copies," Hansen explains. "We consider book requests (loans) but generally can only lend to consortium libraries. For consortium libraries, we ship books using insured FedEx. We require that the materials stay in the library and be used/viewed only in the borrowing library's special collections reading room."

The requests come through interlibrary loan and staff will take them to special collections/archives. Special collections/archives staff retrieve the items and make some of the copies; if too busy they may allow ILL staff to do the scanning in the ILL Copy Center.

The department follows ACRL's *Guidelines for the Interlibrary Loan of Rare and Unique Materials* with the exception of the loan period. "We only give the patron two weeks for use and one week for travel to the library and one week to travel back," explains Hansen. "This is a 30-day checkout period. Also, the ACRL guidelines stipulate that ILL should provide a reason for not lending, but there is no mechanism in OCLC to give a more complete reason other than 'non-circulating'."

"We have seen an increase in requests for items thought to be in our library as a result of our Overland Trails exhibit (the library's first major digitization effort)," Hansen adds.

XI. Measuring Productivity and Evaluating Services

The department runs monthly and annual reports for ILL Borrowing, ILL Lending, and Faculty/Graduate Document Delivery services, and copyright reports (CCG reports) on ILL Borrowing requests for periodical articles. Weekly reports are run to find incomplete requests to guarantee that all requests are completed in a timely fashion. The department also prepares a detailed annual report that breaks down services by patron type and by the type of service received.

"We prepare reports for our consortial partners such as GWLA and the Utah Academic Library Council," says Hansen. "Our library director is especially interested in our GWLA statistics because of the need to meet specific service standards. He is especially interested in meeting or exceeding our ILL Lending turnaround times."

"We use ILLiad reports and customized Access reports using ILLiad data for most measures of productivity. We concentrate on fill ratios and turnaround times. When numbers dip in these rates we analyze our workflow and staffing to see if we can discover problems in training or to change workflow. We also generate reports on consortia based activity and we create reports of our RapidILL activity. We create reports for our state consortia, GWLA and RLG consortia," says Hansen.

"All of our processes in all of our ILL related services are focused on 24-hour or less turnaround within our office. We usually complete any request received within our 10-hour-a-day work schedule and generally get very complimentary comments from our patrons and almost no complaints," Hansen summarizes.

The University of Tennessee

David P. Atkins, Head, Resource Sharing and Document Delivery, John C. Hodges Library

I. Description of The University of Tennessee and Library

The University of Tennessee serves as the flagship campus of the state university system. Founded in 1794 and designated as the state land-grant institution in 1869, the main campus in Knoxville remains the university's largest campus, with 20,000 undergraduate and 6,000 graduate students enrolled in 400 academic programs in 15 schools and colleges.

According to Association of Research Libraries statistics (ARL, 2006-2007), the University of Tennessee Libraries is the 53rd largest ARL research university library (out of 113) and the 29th largest public research university library. In 2007-2008, the University Libraries had a budget of $16.78 million and expenditures (including development funds) of $17.4 million, employed 195 full-time staff including 39 professional librarians and hosted 2.1 million visitors.

The UT Libraries holds more than 2.6 million volumes in the John C. Hodges Library (the centrally located "main library"), the George F. DeVine Music Library, the Webster Pendergrass Agriculture and Veterinary Medicine Library, our special collections (housed in the architecturally significant James D.Hoskins Library) and the Social Work Library (located in Nashville). UT Libraries is known on campus and nationally for innovative uses of technology, including its work with collaborative spaces (Commons, Digital Media Services, The Studio), digital library initiatives, an excellent interlibrary loan system, innovative user education programs and strong user-centered service philosophy. The UT Libraries is viewed as the core intellectual, cultural and social space on the campus.

During the 2007-2008 fiscal year, the UT Libraries borrowed 20,815 items and loaned 30,453 items to other libraries.

II. Description of Staffing and ILL Budget

The following staff comprise the Interlibrary Services Unit: Borrowing Supervisor, Borrowing Associates, Lending Supervisor, Lending Associate and student workers. David Atkins, who is Head of Resource Sharing and Document Delivery, manages the unit.

Head, Resource Sharing and Document Delivery (faculty, 1) leads ILL Borrowing, Lending and several other library departments. He provides strategic management for libraries' ILL/Doc Delivery services and manages ILL systems; participates in librarywide management committees and working groups; and leads local, state and regional resource sharing projects.

Borrowing Supervisor (nonexempt, 1) manages daily operations of ILL Borrowing and Distance Education and hires student employees. The Borrowing Supervisor trains staff and resolves tough, problematic requests referred by other staff.

Borrowing Associates (nonexempt, 2) process ILL requests, coming and going, using OCLC, Rapid and DOCLINE® networks. They assist patrons in-person, on the phone and via email with reference and ILL queries. They supervise assigned student employees and maintain department equipment.

Lending Supervisor (nonexempt, 1) manages daily operations of ILL Lending. Supervisor hires student employees; trains staff; resolves problematic requests referred by other staff; and advises other libraries on access to UT's collections and ILL services.

Lending Associate (nonexempt) processes ILL requests, coming and going, using OCLC, Rapid and DOCLINE® networks. Associate assists other libraries on the phone and via email, and assigned student employees and maintains department equipment.

Staff Education

According to Atkins, "Formal training is ad hoc and opportunistic. For example, if a National Library of Medicine trainer visits our area, some staff may attend a PubMed or DOCLINE® training session. Most training is informal and performed by staff, since the state's library association and state's library consortium seldom offer training supporting ILL."

"However, as part of our new KUDZU IDS interlibrary loan assessment project, for the first time we are using Webinar training hosted by SUNY-Geneseo librarians," Atkins elaborates. "SUNY-Geneseo provides training as part of our KUDZU-IDS pilot project. If successful, we may explore more Web-based opportunities."

Role in Collections and Acquisitions

Atkins also describes the department's role in collections and acquisitions as ad hoc and informal. "There's nothing 'built in' to our CD process that regularly uses ILL data,"

says Atkins. "Of course, if subject libraries request reports or data, we will provide the needed information."

Placement of ILL Department in Library's Organization

Our interlibrary services (ILS) unit combines borrowing and lending. ILS unit is part of a larger department, resource sharing and document delivery (RSSD). RSDD combines ILS, Library Express document delivery, shipping and receiving, main library stacks and the storage facility. RSDD reports to a librarian, the department head, who reports to the assistant dean responsible for branch libraries, assessment and RSDD.

Budget Information

The budget for the RSDD department for fiscal year 2007 includes the following categories and amounts:

Staff (students, nonexempt, faculty): $184,000

Resource Sharing Management: $105,575

Shipping: $ 32,000

Copies/Supplies $ 16,245

Best Management Advice for Other Academic ILL Departments

Atkins offers the following best management advice:

Automate: If a system can automatically perform tasks that are also performed by staff, go for the automation.

Simplify: You may think a policy or workflow saves money, but you actually pay for it with inefficiencies. If you employ policies and rules to control volume and costs, compare the amount you believed you saved with the amount of effort required to enforce or otherwise manage.

Example 1: Lender due dates for books. If you lend books for four weeks and always grant four-week renewals, why not lend the book for eight weeks/no renewals and save both you and the borrower the formality of asking for renewals.

Example 2: If your copy of a book is checked out, don't cancel the ILL and make the patron issue a recall. Order it on ILL. Recalls create all sorts of work for ILL, circulation and the patron with the book, not to mention ill will. You already have one patron who wants that book. You need two copies, so borrow the second. If another library's copy is sitting unused on their shelves, get it for your patron.

III. Software and Automation

The ILS unit uses OCLC ILLiad for borrowing, lending and document delivery. DOCLINE® and Rapid are used with ILLiad connection for borrowing and lending, and Odyssey, Ariel and Adobe for scanning and electronic document delivery.

Electronic Delivery and Software Enhancements

Odyssey/Ariel Lending: Both applications are used to send and receive ILL copies among participating libraries. For lending, staff will either photocopy articles then "feed" copies through scanner autosheet feeder or scan directly from the original. Ariel also supports e-mail delivery for lending and is used extensively to fill e-copy loans to libraries without Ariel.

Odyssey/Ariel Borrowing: Staff review most incoming transmissions for quality and accuracy using ILLiad Electronic Delivery Processing to update requests as received and then deliver to patrons. With Odyssey, UT does use Trusted Sender for several lending partners, bypassing the staff quality check and manual updating.

Adobe: UT scans documents as .PDF for on-campus ILLiad document delivery. UT Borrowing also reformats paper copy ILLs to .PDF for electronic delivery. When copyright appropriate, UT scans entire theses directly to PDF for a fee.

"We've just installed better-quality, faster scanners as an enhancement to improve our Lending's "scan directly from the original" work flow," says Atkins.

Best Management Advice for Other Academic ILL Departments

"For processing orders, OCLC Worldcat Resource Sharing and ILLiad both make for efficient ILL," Atkins advises. "Be sure to use one of these."

"For the foreseeable future, many ILL departments will continue to use both Ariel and Odyssey for electronic document transmission," Atkins predicts. "As more libraries use the no-cost Odyssey stand-alone, Odyssey may replace Ariel as the defacto e-doc delivery standard. If you have Ariel but not ILLiad, you can use Odyssey. Can't beat the price: It's free."

According to Atkins, improved (and affordable) Electronic Resource Management Systems will simply license tracking and streamline ILL Lending use of e-journals for order fulfillment. "Take advantage of these systems when you can," he suggests.

"Anecdotally, 'Next Generation Catalogs' create substantial increases (perhaps spikes) in both interlibrary loan and campus document delivery volume," Atkins adds. "Include these operations in 'next gen' planning, specifically with an eye towards handling increases in request volume."

IV. Resource Sharing Consortia

The John C. Hodges Library participates in the following consortia:

Tennessee Resource Sharing (TRS): Reciprocal borrowing/lending network of Tennessee public and private libraries (school, public, and academic). Participants may use OCLC, email, fax and any other accepted request method to submit requests.

SOLINET: No charge borrowing and lending among SOLINET network members, who also use OCLC ILL. Borrowers may pay for rush services or special delivery requests (e.g. FedEx next day).

KUDZU: Subset of ASERL/SOLINET libraries that provide 24-hour turnaround on lending side and electronic delivery for copies and expedited delivery for loans. Some KUDZU libraries subscribe to a regional courier for deliveries among libraries. Those without the courier subscription use their preferred expedited ground delivery, which varies by institution. Some use UPS, USPS Priority or FedEx.

Rapid: The UT Libraries pays an annual subscription for Rapid, which includes no-charge borrowing and lending of copies among ARL and academic libraries that have subscribed to Rapid and provide Rapid holdings files. All applicable copyright fees are paid by the borrowing library. Participants agree to provide priority services, striving for a 24-hour turnaround on the lending side. Copies are delivered via Ariel.

"KUDZU allows us to use KUDZU courier," Atkins explains. "Our cost per item in FY09 using the KUDZU courier was $1.95 compared to FedEx Lending/UPS Mail Returns' cost of $3.40 per item. Cost comparisons include returning items we borrow to the lending library. KUDZU libraries that do not use the courier, use their choice of FedEx, UPS or USPS Priority mail. Providing 48-hour shipping from lenders to borrowers is one the KUDZU requirements."

"Courier also simplifies shipping tremendously," Atkins adds. "No more laborious packaging. Bag in reusable courier bag then in shipping crate and, boom, we're done. We consistently receive one- and two-day service from our courier."

"Using Rapid in FY08, we received over 9,320 filled articles, costing UT $0.64 per order. Fill rate is regularly between 92-94 percent," says Atkins.

"Reciprocal agreements save money two ways. First, you don't have to pay lenders fees. Second, you don't have to manage invoices (issuing and paying.) Since we receive such excellent service from Rapid and other consortial groups, we often don't get those 'second try' requests. If unable to fill using our groups, we will go to document delivery supplier.

Impact of New Technology on Resource Sharing

The University of Tennessee and the Tennessee State Library and Archives use Z39.50 catalog searching and ISO ILL connectivity to communicate between UT's ILLiad and Auto-Graphic's ILL system. State public libraries may easily order from UT. The library's lending volume to the state increased over 40 percent due to this technology.

V. Commercial Document Delivery

ILL will typically try regular libraries first, then a document supplier. The staff use document suppliers first when the title is not listed in CCC or they refer ILL to the publisher. There are many cases where the British Library is the only source for a title, so staff will order from them.

The library also orders fairly regularly from CISTI, Chemical Abstracts, Ingenta, InfoTrieve, Optipat and SIRC. There are quite a few suppliers that interlibrary services has used just once or twice: AllAcademic, Cinahl, EbscoDoc, Harvard Business Publishing, Instant Information, MathDoc, Northern Lights, NTIS, Sociological Abstracts and Storming Media, for example. Interlibrary services does not track the fees. If the charges are more than the maximum cost allowed, staff will ask if the patron wants to continue with the request.

Unmediated or Mediated Access to Document Delivery Services

Interlibrary services only offers mediated access to document suppliers at this time.

Fee-Based Services

The lending department does charge fees for loans and articles to borrowers outside our reciprocal and consortial agreements.

VI. Copyright and Licensing

ILL Copyright-Compliant Policy or Guidelines

ILS follows the CONTU "Rule of Five" and uses ILLiad to track copyright. As staff process article orders, they also record copyright information using ILLiad "Copyright Clearance." The institution maintains a deposit account and ILS staff episodically submit Copyright Clearance Center reports for payment. As the account is drawn down, staff will request invoices to replenish the account.

Best Management Advice for Other Academic ILL Departments

"Consider acquiring copies via document delivery suppliers whose fees include copyright charges," Atkins advises.

Major ILL Copyright and Licensing Issues

Atkins sees securing ILL rights for e-journals as a major licensing issue. "It takes more effort to manage," he says. "E-journal articles make for quicker lending since no physical items need be handled. It also points the way for publishers and their agents to eventually replace ILL Lending. Borrowers would go directly to publisher or doc delivery provider, bypassing ILL Lending."

The library's electronic subscriptions do include provisions for lending, but according to Atkins, "Rights will vary by publisher."

"We advise collection development and serials/technical services on the need to maintain ILL rights," Atkins reports. "We also advise on technical requirements for ILL rights management within electronic resource management systems."

VII. Institutional Repositories and Open Access

"We do not include Open Access tools in discovery," says Atkins. "We rely on OPAC and Google searching. We also benefit from Rapid networks 'Unmediated Lending' that automatically fills requests if 'fillable' by OA sources. Rapid ILL network includes OA holdings along with participant library holdings. So, if a Rapid request can be filled by OA, Rapid makes the connection and 'supplies' the copy."

"We haven't integrated OA/IR sources into our workflows enough to gauge their impact on total operations," Atkins adds.

VIII. Service Priorities for Constituents

Interlibrary services does not distinguish between students, faculty and staff in terms of ILL policies. ILS does not limit patrons to a maximum number of requests and will provide services at no cost up to $35 per order. If an order costs more than $35, the patron may be asked to pay the difference. The department discourages ordering textbooks.

ILL Services for Community Members, Visiting Scholars or Other Institutions

"We provide ILL services to any visiting scholar or any other designee which receives sponsorship by a UT department or unit," relates Atkins. "UT departments may confer a temporary UT affiliation to individuals. This service is managed by our campus' Office of Information Technology. They register these guests in our campus online directory (LDAP). Once in the directory, any individual may use ILL, circulation and remote database/e-journal access."

Special Services to Constituents

ILL coordinates with Library Express, the campus document delivery service, to have ILL loans delivered and picked up across campus. ILL also provides no charge loan and copy services for distance education (DE) students and faculty.

"Occasionally, interviews may happen in person or over the phone. ILL staff usually provide registration and 'how to use ILL' point-of-use training. Preferred practice is to refer reference questions to our reference department," says Atkins.

Notification and Delivery of Materials

Patrons are notified by email, regular mail and occasionally by phone. Materials may be picked up at the main or at two branch libraries (Music and Agriculture-Veterinary Medicine). On-campus faculty, graduate students and staff are eligible for campus delivery. Registered distance education students and faculty receive no charge FedEx for all loans. DE patrons are responsible for returning items.?

IX. Services to Distance Learning Students

"In 2001, we established combined ILL/document delivery services for DE patrons," reports Atkins. "As the library dedicated a librarian and at one point a staff person to provide DE services, we integrated ILL/document delivery into the package."

"DE requests look just like regular requests until we receive the item," Atkins explains. "Our ILL system flags the loan for special DE processing. DE patrons receive document delivery of locally held items. Registered distance ed students and faculty receive no change FedEx for all loans (local or ILL). DE patrons are responsible for returning items. In FY08, we served 144 DE students and faculty."

According to Atkins, no special purchases have been made to support interlibrary services for distance education. These services have integrated well with the department's traditional ILL/Doc Del processes. "DE learners, however, receive no-cost copies of locally held materials. Local patrons pay for that service," Atkins says.

X. Special Collections

The library does not loan special collection items. Interlibrary services for special collections is limited to copying and scanning, and special collections staff determine if the item can physically withstand reproduction. "Our special collections department works with our interlibrary loan department. They also field requests directly from the public," states Atkins.

XI. Measuring Productivity and Evaluating Services

"We primarily use custom MS Access queries of our ILLiad ILL/Document delivery system," Atkins explains. "I run reports for monthly and annual summaries, historical review, and any other time the library administration or myself need data." Reports include orders submitted, filled; identifying lenders and borrowers, copies vs. loans, patron demographics, and orders routed between ILL and Document Delivery. As a CCC participant, Interlibrary services also uses ILLiad's CCC reports when they pay copyright. Staff must review the report for accuracy, making sure to exclude titles owned or otherwise not subject to the CONTU guidelines.

"As a Rapid Library, we rely on Rapid to provide monthly lending performance data, such as orders processed and filled, and turnaround time," says Atkins. "As a KUDZU network library, we rely on our courier vendor to provide delivery performance data. KUDZU is also working with IDS (Information Delivery Services Project) from SUNY Geneseo to pilot use of the IDS ILL performance tracking data collection system."

"We've used turnaround time to identify areas in need of improvement," says Atkins. "This subsequently leads to discussions on workflows and how to improve. In lending, e-copies were delivered via Ariel, but the orders not updated to shipped until some time, even hours, after shipped. This leads to low turnaround time and real problems receiving OCLC or Rapid credit for filled requests."

"UT participated in the last two ARL LibQual surveys," Atkins adds. "We also post an informal Web questionnaire on ILL and Doc Del Web sites and our ILLiad Web page to help evaluate services."

Colorado State University

Cristi MacWaters, Interlibrary Loan Coordinator, Colorado State University Libraries

I. Description of Colorado State University and Library

Colorado State University is one of our nation's leading research universities with world-class research in infectious disease, atmospheric science, clean energy technologies, and environmental science. It was founded in 1870 as the Colorado Agricultural College, six years before the Colorado Territory became a state. Last year, CSU awarded degrees to more than 5,000 graduates, and this year, it attracted nearly $300 million in research funding. Colorado State is a land-grant institution and a Carnegie Doctoral/Research University-Extensive.

The Colorado State University Libraries is a land grant ARL library. The libraries currently house approximately 2 million volumes, 31,300 serial titles and access to 24,000 online journals. The libraries serve approximately 25,000 students and 5,000 faculty and staff.

The CSU Libraries borrowed 66,485 items and loaned 70,733 items during the 2008 calendar year.

II. Description of Staffing and ILL Budget

All staff are paraprofessionals and comprise: the department head, the borrowing unit head and two staff, the lending unit head and two staff and student workers.

The department head trains and supervises and evaluates the two unit heads, represents the department on various library committees and is part of the management team, and sits on the Rapid development team. Currently the department head also fills six hours staffing the information commons service desk. The department head provides statistical reports to the collection management team on a semiannual basis and to liaisons on demand, collects statistical data that is reported annually for ARL stats and other uses. This position travels to ALA twice a year, attends the Colorado ILL workshop, the annual GWLA resource sharing meeting and Prospector (our INNREACH consortium) committee meetings two or three times a year.

The Borrowing/Local Document Delivery unit has three staff. The borrowing unit supervisor hires and trains student workers, supervises, trains and evaluates two staff members working under her. She also staffs the information commons service desk at least six hours a week.

The two staff positions in the borrowing unit manage day-to-day workflow of borrowing and local document delivery services. Students comprise a large part of the workforce in the interlibrary loan unit, so these positions ensure that there is appropriate work available for student employees as they come to work each day, prioritizing tasks as the day develops. One position specializes in ALA requests, ensuring that the invoices are prepared for the library business office, and is the overdue notice "enforcer" in addition to routine search/sending responsibilities in OCLC and on Rapid, and meets customer service needs arising during the day. The other position supervises the processing of materials received on our INNREACH service -- 75 percent of our book requests are filled through this service -- and also posts articles received via OCLC to patrons' ILLiad accounts in addition to search/sending responsibilities in OCLC and on Rapid and handling customer service questions.

The lending unit supervisor oversees total workflow and is the point of contact for scanner software maintenance and upgrades. He fills at least six hours at the information commons service desk, oversees two full-time staff members in training and evaluation, hires and trains student employees. Student workers do most of the physical pulling and scanning, processing and mailing. Two staff positions evaluate article requests to ensure that if we fill from an electronic journal, we are licensed to do so. They evaluate requests to make sure the requests are charged appropriately if the library is not a member of one of our consortia, and they process incoming payments for libraries we have invoiced. Staff make sure that all incoming OCLC and INNREACH requests are processed and updated each day.

Staff Education

"We encourage all staff members to join appropriate listservs such as ILL-L, Ariel-L, ILLiad, Rapid, to monitor any developments in interlibrary loan," says MacWaters. "Colorado hosts a very fine interlibrary loan workshop every April and we make sure all full-time staff attend it. The library and university hold training on various productivity suite software that staff are expected to attend. When there is a major upgrade to ILL software, the companies usually sponsor online classes about the upgrade and we make sure to attend these as well. Staff are occasionally asked to present at other venues on programs we are doing at CSU. For example, the borrowing supervisor was asked to participate on a panel on our buy vs. borrow program (Purchase Direct) at the Mountain and Plains Library Association meeting."

Role in Collections and Acquisitions

The department provides detailed statistics for copyright royalties paid for journal titles to influence purchase decisions, and books borrowed that may need to be purchased. The department provides usage statistics to inform cancellation decisions.

Placement of ILL Department in Library's Organization

Interlibrary loan stands as its own department reporting to the assistant dean for the learning commons, who reports to the dean of libraries.

Budget Information

The ILL department budget for fiscal year 2007 consisted of the following amounts:

OCLC	$122,700
ILL Management Software	$7,000
IFM Borrowing payments	$63,000
IFM Lending Receipts	$35,320
Invoiced payments to Lending libraries	$28,000
Invoiced charges to Borrowing Libraries	$6,925
Staff Salaries	$513,000
Student Wages	$69,000
Courier Service	$10,250
Postage	$65,000
Scanner Maintenance	$6,000
Total	$841,705

III. Software and Automation

The department uses ILLiad for borrowing. "We are migrating from CLIO to Relays for lending," MacWaters reports. "We use an INNREACH service for much of book lending/borrowing. We use Rapid for the majority of our article borrowing/lending. At this point, OCLC is really a minority of our business."

Electronic Delivery and Software Enhancements

The department uses Ariel for desktop delivery. Staff post articles received to patrons' ILLiad accounts or forward PDFs received from libraries sent to the staff email account. "On the lending side, we will be using Relais Express scanning software, which will allow us to deliver via Odyssey, Ariel, email, fax, or post to Web all through one software," MacWaters explains. "If a library does not have Ariel, we almost always are able to use Ariel to send the article to an email account."

Description of Rapid:

The CSU Libraries are a leader in resource sharing due to the Rapid article delivery service. Rapid enables peer-to-peer sharing of articles in an efficient, fast and cost effective manner. CSU has built a union catalog of library holdings participants can easily contribute to. Rapid requires at least semiannual holdings updates, though libraries are encouraged to send holdings more often. Libraries are encouraged to send all their holdings to enable the borrowing staff to easily identify locally held requests. From that set of holdings, Rapid can suppress any holdings that a library cannot or does not want to lend; for example, e-journals not licensed for ILL, formats that do not copy well (microfilm, art journals) or holdings at locations that may be difficult to service (branch libraries, storage facilities.) Libraries are expected to either fill or update to unfilled within 24 hours.

Requests are submitted by ILL staff to Rapid. The system matches on year and ISSN or OCLC number and routes the request to a lending library. The routing is load leveled by the system looking at which library owning this item has had the fewest requests at that moment. Lending libraries receive a request that has their call number and location embedded on the request. The transaction number and Ariel IP (soon to be Odyssey IP) are also bar-coded. The request should need no further searching in the lending office. It is not a burden for libraries to fill within 24 hoursbecause they are only receiving requests for material they have identified that they own, and the request comes with the call number already in place.

"CSU has seen the percentage of our article traffic filled by Rapid increase over the past few years from 60 percent of articles requested filled on Rapid to 78 percent this past year. System wide, Rapid averages a 90-95 percent fill rate with a turnaround time of about 16 hours from the time the request is placed in the system until it is updated to filled by a supplying library. CSU recently calculated that borrowing articles cost about $6.32 per article. Our costs would have been much higher without the Rapid service."

"There are two new innovations Rapid has implemented in the past year," says MacWaters. "The first is the ability to do unmediated borrowing of articles. Rapid software can poll the ILLiad queue of Awaiting Request Processing articles and route them as appropriate. Since the majority of our requests come in from our databases through an open URL resolver (SFX in our case), they come in with the complete citation and an ISSN. These meet the criteria for Rapid searching so the program polls this queue, identifies requests that can be filled locally, requests that can be filled by Rapid, requests that are duplicates of requests made by the same patron, and requests that can't be filled by Rapid and need to be sent on OCLC. Since around 60-70 percent of our article requests come in through the databases, the bulk of our article requests can go through without staff intervention. The remaining requests that only need an ISSN can be handled with minimal intervention. Staff apply the ISSN and return the request to the queue, where the system will pick it up the next time the queue is polled."

The second innovation is the creation and use of a database of open access journal articles. Rapid staff harvest open access article archives that are indexed to the article level. Primarily the archives are DOAJ and PubMed Central, and Open J-Gate. Staff also harvest institutional repositories that Rapid members alert Rapid staff to access. When a request is submitted by the borrower to the Rapid system, the system first checks the open access article database and if a match is made down to the title level, the article is retrieved from the database and Arieled to the borrowing library. While the amount of article requests filled this way is not large yet, Rapid has hopes that it will continue to grow. The turnaround time for articles that are filled in this manner, however, is impressive. It averages around seven minutes from the time the request is submitted until it is available on the patron's desktop.

IV. Resource Sharing Consortia

The CSU Libraries is a member of the Colorado Alliance for Research Libraries, Greater Western Library Alliance, and recently joined LVIS (Libraries Very Interested in Sharing) in hopes of further reducing borrowing fees. CSU Libraries founded the Rapid system.

"Consortium buying power indirectly impacts ILL service by allowing us to acquire better e-journal packages than we'd ordinarily be able to provide," says MacWaters, citing one advantage to consortia.

"Our consortia provide free service to other members. In addition, GWLA has strict performance standards for its members so delivery is very fast among members," continues MacWaters. "Rapid specializes in article delivery and also has high service expectations. While members pay a membership fee to participate, there are no lending fees and many members extend reciprocity to other areas such as OCLC borrowing."

V. Commercial Document Delivery

The ILL department purchases a lot of pre-pub/e-pub articles for patrons. With the increasing amount of electronic-only journals and with publishers frequently placing embargoes on the most current year, the amount of article purchasing has increased dramatically.

The department uses CISTI, British Library and Chemical Abstracts occasionally, if they are the only holders of the journal. "We sometimes use these services when CCC is not licensed to collect royalties on a journal. These services include copyright fees as part of their charge. We have set up a custom holdings path on OCLC to automate this process," says MacWaters.

Unmediated or Mediated Access to Document Delivery Services

"Document delivery services are mediated, and we don't use them often. We do not have limits on material ordered," states MacWaters.

VI. Copyright and Licensing

ILL Copyright-Compliant Policy or Guidelines

The department uses ILLiad to track copyright titles. Staff pay the Copyright Clearance Center via the ILLiad interface to submit copyright orders to CCC. Being part of the GWLA consortium, CSU Libraries has negotiated a lower service fee from CCC. The department pays CCC invoices with a credit card.

Best Management Advice for Other Academic ILL Departments

"Sometimes buying articles directly from a publisher's Web site can be cheaper than paying CCC service fee and royalties," advises MacWaters. "For example, Nature Protocols is $35 copyright plus service fees from CCC. If you buy from the publisher's Web site the charge is between $18-$32."

Licensing Strategies

"We don't sign licenses unless ILL is allowed," states MacWaters. "Our contracts and licensing staff are well aware of our needs and argue for the best language possible. Many of our e-journals are licensed through consortia (GWLA or Colorado Alliance), which strengthens our position to negotiate with the publisher."

VII. Institutional Repositories and Open Access

Rapid has created an OA and IR database for searching for these materials (see complete description listed above in III. *Software and Automation*).

VIII. Service Priorities for Constituents

"We treat all our users -- undergraduates, graduate students and faculty -- the same," MacWaters says. "We put the same effort in obtaining their requests and verifying their citations. They all have the same loan period on returnable items. We don't do rush requests for anyone as we manage to get all but the most esoteric requests out to a potential supplier the same day the request is made."

ILL Services for Community Members, Visiting Scholars or Other Institutions

Interlibrary loan is available to CSU faculty, staff and students only. Visiting scholars with some connection to a university department will be eligible for interlibrary loan/local document delivery services. If members of some other local institution (a U.S. Forest Service station, for example) have an affiliation with a CSU academic department, they will be eligible for service. However, if they don't have an affiliation with CSU, they will need to use their institutional service.

Special Services to Constituents

ILL provides local document delivery to all CSU-affiliated users for free. If a user makes a request for something owned by the CSU libraries, staff will retrieve the book and place it on the pickup shelves at the circulation desk or mail it to them depending on their delivery preference specified in ILLiad. Staff will scan and deliver print articles to their desktop. If their request is available from our electronic journal collection, staff will download the article and email it to them.

The department also has a program called Purchase Direct. ILL will route book requests out of the ILL workflow to the acquisitions workflow based on the following criteria: not owned by CSU and published in the last five years. This is accomplished by a routing rule in ILLiad so staff intervention is not required. The requests route into a queue in ILLiad called Awaiting Acquisitions Processing. The Head of Acquisitions examines all the requests in this queue, and if the item is scholarly in nature, quickly available and under a certain dollar threshold, she will buy the item for our collection. The libraries receive most items within a few days. The item is quickly cataloged and made available to the requesting patron.

Notification and Delivery of Materials

"We have mailed items to patrons at their request starting in 1997 as a result of the flood," says MacWaters. "For six months or so, everything had to be mailed since they could not pick up materials at the library. Once we moved back in the building, we gave patrons the option to have their materials mailed, to pick up at the main library or to pick up at our veterinary or atmospheric science branch libraries. Patrons are emailed automatically if they are picking up their material at a library. If we are mailing their material, we do not do an additional email to say we are mailing their materials."

IX. Services to Distance Learning Students

The department has offered services to distance users since distance education started at CSU 15 years ago. The department offers distance education users the same services as other constituents.

"We have never been able to get distance students or our remote faculty to reliably self identify, and this was part of the impetus behind mailing books to those who request our services," MacWaters mentions. "We make no distinction between DE and other requests. The only difference for DE students is that we use UPS for delivery out of the Front Range area (Fort Collins-Pueblo). So if the user lives out of state or the other side of the mountains, we use UPS to make sure they get two-day delivery."

"When we mail books to anyone, distance or otherwise, we only pay postage to the user," MacWaters adds. "It is up to them to return the book to us. Most of them walk it in or return in campus mail. For DE students, it is up to them to return the book to us. They may use USPS, UPS, statewide courier or have someone return it to us."

X. Special Collections

The ILL department lends a limited amount of special collections material. "The special collections people make the decision about lending out the material," says MacWaters. "We usually lend CSU materials from the university archives or natural resources material, although some fiction in the past has been loaned. We prefer to scan rather than lend out physical copies. We have a Bookeye scanner, and both ILL and special collections staff will do the scanning." Special collections is making efforts to digitize their collections to make material more visible and available to patrons without having to place ILL requests.

The department encourages patrons to request special collections material through ILLiad. ILL will process and ship items using UPS for tracking purposes and will require the borrowing institution to limit use to the library. The department follows the ACRL *Guidelines for the Interlibrary Loan of Rare and Unique Materials* for lending out items from special collections.

XI. Measuring Productivity and Evaluating Services

The department generates ILLiad statistics for annual ARL reporting purposes. Most of the requested material goes through Rapid, which requires a 24-hour time commitment. Turnaround time is monitored by Rapid staff, and performance spreadsheets with measures are made available by staff to Rapid participants.

"We have done LibQual in the past, the last survey was conducted in 2005, and we will be scheduling another LibQual survey," notes MacWaters. "ILL consistently rates as highly valued service. We also participated in the Mary Jackson ARL survey assessment of ILL performance, published in 2004 with data from 2002. When we looked at how much local document delivery cost, it turned out to be about 50 cents per item. We decided to enhance services by implementing document delivery to our CSU faculty, staff, and student constituents."

GWLA (Greater Western Library Association) conducts a performance study twice a year, and participants agree to lend 85percent of their articles within two OCLC referral days, and books within three days. CSU is evaluated, and MacWaters reviews these performance measures.

Oberlin College

Diane Lee, Interlibrary Loan Supervisor, The Oberlin College Library

I. Description of Oberlin College and Library

"Oberlin College uniquely combines a four-year liberal arts college and conservatory of music. Our community is known for academic and musical excellence and its commitment to social engagement and diversity.

The College of Arts and Sciences offers a four-year undergraduate program leading to the Bachelor of Arts degree and provides a rich and balanced curriculum in the humanities, social sciences, and natural sciences. The College also offers a 12-month graduate course of study leading to the Master of Education degree. Since 1920, more Oberlin graduates have gone on to earn PhDs than have graduates of any other American baccalaureate college."

Oberlin College. "Apply to Oberlin < http://new.oberlin.edu/applying/>. March 2009.

"Students at Oberlin have access to superior library resources. The recipient of a prestigious award for excellence in academic libraries, the Oberlin College Library has one of the largest and finest undergraduate collections in the nation. The Main Library, housed in Mudd Center, remains busy with academic and social activities and its recently opened Academic Commons encourages community and collaboration. In addition, three specialized libraries are devoted to art, music, and science. All four libraries offer strong collections, extensive electronic access to databases and journals, and excellent reference staff. Total holdings for the library system exceed 2.3 million items. In addition, the OhioLINK consortium provides access to more than 46 million volumes from 87 institutions in Ohio."

Oberlin College. "Oberlin College Library" < http://new.oberlin.edu/arts-and-sciences/libraries/>. March 2009.

The Oberlin College Library borrowed 17,625 and loaned 44,413 items in 2006-2007.

II. Description of Staffing and ILL Budget

The circulation department (which includes ILL) consists of the Head of Circulation, the Interlibrary Loan Supervisor and seven Interlibrary Loan Assistants.

Head of Circulation: Supervises all other regular Circulation/ILL staff.

Interlibrary Loan Supervisor: Responsible for daily ILL activity and supervision of student employees. Responsible for lending and borrowing sides of ILL, processes incoming and outgoing requests, generates reports, locates difficult-to-find items and works with constituents to resolve problems or questions on a daily basis.

Interlibrary Loan Assistants (7): Students responsible for paging, processing, photocopying, packing unpacking materials.

Staff Education

Individual supervisors train their student staff. All Oberlin College Library regular staff members are encouraged to locate and attend staff development opportunities.

"I will be attending ALA in Chicago this summer and plan to go to the ILLiad users group sessions," Lee reports. "I also have attended the OhioLink resource sharing conferences in the past."

Role in Collections and Acquisitions

"We regularly assess ILL requests we get for their appropriateness for our collection and occasionally recommend purchase," says Lee. "Upon request, we can provide our collection development staff with historical information."

Placement of ILL Department in Library's Organization

Interlibrary loan is part of the circulation department. The Head of Circulation reports to the library director.

Budget Information

"Our ILL costs are folded in with other services we pay for to our OCLC regional service provider. Supplies and mailing costs are not tracked separately," Lee says.

Best Management Advice for Other Academic ILL Departments

Lee recommends obtaining materials from free consortial resources. "Our custom holdings are set up to receive electronic first rather than paper, and are set up to receive the free articles first. The free OhioLink libraries appear first, and are sent via Odyssey/Ariel, and the next category is the reciprocal libraries, like the Oberlin Group, and these are also free. We are always trying to save money and to cut down on the amount of paper for sending articles."

When sending items, Lee recommends using FedEx or the U.S. Postal Service, using the online form to save time and to print out mailing labels. "Also, if too many materials are getting lost in the mail, consider sending ILL materials traceable even though it may cost a little more," Lee advises.

III. Software and Automation

The department relies exclusively on ILLiad for resource sharing software. "We currently send scanned articles through Ariel, and receive through Odyssey and Ariel (we plan to go live sending Odyssey this summer)," Lee says. "Staff retrieve articles from the stacks and then scan and send them using Ariel. Items received via Ariel are imported into ILLiad, and then get posted as a PDF on the patrons account. I look at all articles using ILLiad Electronic Delivery Processing to make sure all pages are there and to check articles received as a batch. Sometimes we have to pull out the print invoices – we don't want our patrons to see invoices and feel that they have to pay for them." Articles are kept up for the semester using the Oberlin server.

The Oberlin College Library uses the 7.3 version of ILLiad. "I like the speed at which I can place requests and also for filling requests, I have a version of Passport that interfaces with ILLiad so I can look up Oberlin items; so that saves time," Lee says. Lee has high praise for many of the ILLiad client features, especially the ability to easily produce lists of pending requests, specific patron requests or material type requests.

IV. Resource Sharing Consortia

The Oberlin College Library participates in both OhioLINK and Oberlin Group for reciprocal and priority lending and provision of articles.

The Oberlin College Library participates in OhioLink, a state-funded consortium of Ohio university and college libraries and the State Library of Ohio. Students, faculty members and staff members affiliated with OhioLINK institutions can request books online, view journal articles online, search authoritative databases and make use of other OhioLINK services that enhance research and education.

"OhioLink allows patrons of any OhioLink library to request items be sent to any other OhioLink library, regardless of whether they are registered patrons of the receiving library," Lee explains. "These requests are handled the same as other requests, and there is no fee. OhioLink uses U.S. Cargo Company to deliver materials and has several sorting centers throughout the state. This really saves shipping costs." Lee reports being happy with the courier service, and materials come in three to five days.

"The Oberlin Group is a group of 80 libraries, and it started in 1984-85 with 50 libraries, for select private colleges to work together, in a variety of ways...all Oberlin Group libraries lend materials for free to each other," Lee explains. "Libraries with exceptionally good collections participate, including Amherst, Barnard, Williams, Vassar, Wesleyan, to list a few. We have access to their collections, which are extensive. The Oberlin College Library is not small, and with over two million items the other Oberlin Group libraries benefit from our collections as well."

Lee reports going out of the state of Ohio to get materials using the Oberlin Group when it is faster. The fastest articles are from those libraries that send via Odyssey.

Lee cites the following advantages for consortial participation: fast turn-around time, free materials, less use of commercial document delivery and high quality control for electronic articles. "We also use some large public library systems, where we can get popular fiction, for example, using our OhioLink consortium. Through OhioLink and Oberlin Group combined we can meet most of our borrowing needs," notes Lee.

V. Commercial Document Delivery

When material is unavailable from other sources, the department will use a commercial document delivery provider. According to Lee, "Ingenta is our primary provider. After that, we'll use whichever source we find it in first. Our collection development staff manages the Ingenta budget. The other services are used occasionally and don't have a major impact on our budget."

Unmediated or Mediated Access to Document Delivery Services

The ILL department offers unmediated access to Ingenta for faculty. "We haven't seen a need to impose limits on amounts ordered," states Lee. In some cases, staff will order the material for faculty using Ingenta (when appropriate), when these requests come through the ILLiad request form.

Fee-Based Services

The Oberlin College Library will charge $10 for any request if a reciprocal agreement is not in place. The ILL department will also borrow from consortia or libraries that charge fees, but does this only if cannot be obtained for free.

VI. Copyright and Licensing

ILL Copyright-Compliant Policy or Guidelines

The ILL department uses the CONTU "Rule of Five" guideline for maintaining copyright compliance. Requested items appear in an awaiting copyright clearance queue, and ILLiad automatically tracks items exceeding the guidelines. The department pays the Copyright Clearance Center for copyright fees.

Major ILL Copyright and Licensing Issues

Libraries with electronic-only subscriptions to resources are often not able to provide copies. If we are unable to find a commercial source for the item, it is essentially unavailable to our users. This has a serious impact on their ability to do research and generate new knowledge.

The Oberlin College Library, both individually and through OhioLink and Oberlin Group, negotiates for electronic subscriptions to be available for lending.

VII. Institutional Repositories and Open Access

According to Lee, the ILL department relies on the OPAC and information in OCLC records to identify open access journals. The department does not track or keep statistics for open access materials.

"They are delivered to our users usually by our providing them with information to access it themselves," states Lee. "There hasn't been a significant reduction in our requesting due to open access."

VIII. Service Priorities for Constituents

Interlibrary loan services are available for Oberlin College students, faculty, staff, and faculty and staff spouses. With the exception of unmediated faculty access to Ingenta, service is the same for students and faculty, and the department does not limit the number of requests. There is no fee for routine requests made by Oberlin College students, staff, faculty, affiliated scholars or members of Friends of the Oberlin College Library. "We do, however, charge $2 for each RUSH request for photocopies/articles for our faculty and students," Lee reports.

ILL Services for Community Members, Visiting Scholars or Other Institutions

People who live or work in Oberlin are eligible to use the ILL service, provided they first become registered borrowers. People who are registered users at OhioLINK libraries, and those with a library account at Cuyahoga County Public Library (Cleveland area) and Westerville Public Library (Columbus area), have access to a virtual statewide library. Through the OhioLINK Library Catalog, books and some audiovisual materials that are not available locally can be requested from other member libraries "Patrons who are not affiliated with Oberlin College may be charged a fee for each interlibrary loan request. Fees are determined by the lender and can range from $3 to $50 per item. Library staff will contact borrowers for authorization before ordering materials with fees exceeding $10," Lee explains.

Special Services to Constituents

According to Lee, the department does not require patrons to consult with reference before placing an ILL request, but reference and circulation staff are always available for consultation.

Notification and Delivery of Materials

Email notifications are sent whenever possible, and those patrons without email are notified via telephone. Materials are made available for pick-up at the Main Library Circulation Desk, although articles can be delivered electronically or in the mail. Article delivery preferences are set up by the patron in ILLiad.

IX. Services to Distance Learning Students

Oberlin has only one campus and does not offer distance learning. However, Oberlin College Library patrons studying outside of Oberlin, including abroad, may request articles be delivered electronically. It does not deliver any other materials off campus. "Electronic article delivery for these students is handled no differently than articles delivered to students, faculty or staff on campus," Lee mentions. "About 100 students each semester are studying off campus. They are studying in traditional academic programs, however, that usually have their own library resources."

X. Special Collections

"We rarely lend special collections items but will provide photocopies of articles -- or whole items when copying does not violate copyright – and only when our Special collections librarian determines that copying will not damage the item in any way," says Lee. "Interlibrary loan staff initially receives all requests and then routes requests to other library departments and branches, including special collections. Special collections and branch libraries pull materials, make copies as necessary and send everything to Main Library ILL staff for remaining processing and shipping."

"We have microfilmed some items that are frequently requested and make those reels available as regular library materials," adds Lee. "Those reels are generally loaned as nonrenewable."

XI. Measuring Productivity and Evaluating Services

"We use reports generated by OCLC (for traditional ILL) and OhioLINK (for in-state direct borrowing) to calculate annual statistics," Lee states. "We have used LibQual and turnaround time statistics from ILLiad for periodical assessment. We are always looking for ways to improve fill rates and turnaround time."

"Now rush status is almost unnecessary because most articles come in two-three days, or sometimes even the same day," says Lee. "If we order an article in the morning, we can receive it that afternoon. Sometimes it can be counterproductive to request a rush status because some libraries don't offer rush services, and send the request on to another library. We know that many of the libraries will send in a day or two without rush status." According to Lee, the department usually receives a lot of positive feedback expressing appreciation for finding items, especially the speed at which articles are delivered.

Stony Brook University

Susan P. Lieberthal, Head, Interlibrary Loan and Business Librarian, Stony Brook University Libraries

I. Description of Stony Brook University and Library

Stony Brook University is one of the four flagship research universities of the State University of New York. The University, located 60 miles east of New York City on Long Island, has 1,900 faculty, more than 23,000 students, and offers 61 majors and 68 minors. The university comprises three colleges and eight schools.

Stony Brook University Libraries is a member of the Association of Research Libraries. The university libraries contain over 2 million books as well as a government depository and a patent depository. The library subscribes to approximately 250 databases with over 63,000 unique electronic journals. The branches of the library are the Main Library, Science and Engineering Library, which incorporates Computer Science, Chemistry, School of Marine and Atmospheric Sciences. The Health Sciences Library is located on a separate campus and is an independent entity.

Stony Brook University Libraries borrowed 11,106 items and loaned 12,930 during fiscal year 2008.

II. Description of Staffing and ILL Budget

The ILL department employs the following staff: Head of Interlibrary Loan Department, Instructional Support Technician, Instructional Support Specialist and three Library Clerks.

Head of ILL Department: The head of the department manages staff, some technical issues like changes to the Web pages, the budget, and initiates new and enhanced ideas for service.

Instructional Support Technician 3: Bibliographic searcher for most of the borrowing requests.

Instructional Support Specialist SL 4: Manages office, assists with borrowing requests and manages document delivery requests.

Library Clerk II: Manages student workers involved in lending requests.

Library Clerk II: Manages student workers, all of lending requests.

Library Clerk II: Manages mail, incoming borrowing requests and return of borrowed items. Greets and helps patrons who come into the ILL office for pick-ups, questions or to drop off items for return to lending library.

Staff Education

Instructional specialists can attend local meetings on a case-by-case basis.

Role in Collections and Acquisitions

"On the borrowing side, we have a small purchase-on-demand program managed by the Head of ILL and the primary borrowing professional," says Lieberthal. "When a hard-to-find item is available at a reasonable cost through Amazon.com or Alibris.com or some other online vendor, and we feel it will add to the collection, we will purchase the item. This saves time as we don't have to request it over and over through OCLC. It also produces the item in a timely manner for the patron. However we only do this if the item is not too expensive, very hard to obtain on OCLC and would enhance our collection. We do not involve selectors, acquisitions or cataloging until after the item has been returned to the ILL office. Then it goes to cataloging to be added to the collection. We do sometimes involve acquisitions, and they are able to rush order items."

Placement of ILL Department in Library's Organization

The ILL department is a separate department loosely allied with public services. All borrowing, lending and document delivery processes are handled in one office.

Budget Information

The ILL department spent the following amount in fiscal year 2007:

Copyright Clearance Center:	$11,018.74
British Library Account:	$1,500
Individual libraries:	$2,468.15
Atlas Systems, maintenance fee and hosting of server:	$7900
Purchase-on-Demand and Document Delivery Suppliers:	$4,400
Staffing	
Regular full-time staff	$282,088
Student costs	$10,286

Best Management Advice for Other Academic ILL Departments

Lieberthal advises libraries to do some purchasing-on-demand. "Set up a debit account with a certain amount of money," Lieberthal suggests, "and use this card to buy items that will take a long time to find through OCLC but are available for a reasonable price through an online bookseller. Purchase-on-demand can only work if it is quick, with not much time to check with selectors, or time to acquire and catalog items until after the item is returned. Some libraries do have a quick system involving selectors, acquisitions and cataloging and that may be the best practice way to do purchase-on-demand. There is no perfect way, whatever works best at your institution."

"Use Loansome Doc for medical items," advises Lieberthal. "Set up a deposit account with your local medical school. That way you can apply fair use copyright rules instead of purchasing items from a document supplier and paying copyright for every item. If the item is in PubMed, you can order it through your Loansome Doc account."

III. Software and Automation

"We use ILLiad exclusively," reports Lieberthal. "We deliver and receive via Ariel or Odyssey. We will mail items out or even fax them for libraries which borrow from us. The enhancement of Odyssey has improved our workflow and speed of completing requests on the lending side. We also have switched on 'Trusted lender' feature in ILLiad on the borrowing side. This feature assumes you trust the quality of work the lending library is sending to you and the electronic item is received, converted to PDF, delivered to the Web and the patron is notified without any intervention from our ILL staff."

IV. Resource Sharing Consortia

"We don't have our main consortium 'set in stone' but most of our lending and borrowing activity is with our other SUNY research centers (University of Buffalo, Binghamton University, University at Albany)," Lieberthal explains. "Our other close consortial partners are Syracuse University, the New York State Library and all the SUNY colleges. We do not charge each other for anything and use a courier service for delivery of items to and from each other's ILL departments. Our SUNY partners are the bulk of our borrowing and lending requests. It is a great way to share collections."

"We use the Center for Research Library (CRL) whenever possible because we pay a very steep fee for membership, and we try to maximize our use of their collection. We also participate in SHARES, originally set up by the RLG. This consortium is committed to providing each member with hard to find items, speedy delivery via UPS and quick turnaround. SHARES helps us with our difficult research requests. We also provide hard to find items, journals, microfilms, music scores, etc. to our SHARES partners. Having SHARES join up with OCLC has improved workflow."

V. Commercial Document Delivery

"We use a document delivery supplier when that is the best practice," Lieberthal reports. "Some items are just not available anywhere else and we have to use a document supplier. We will do whatever it takes to obtain items for users, but we only use a document supplier when it is not easily available elsewhere. When we receive a request from *Chemical Abstracts* we order the full text and pay for it. We also order from the British Library, CISTI and individual publications. We only purchase items that we can pay for using our credit card. We reconcile once a month. Items being billed on the lending side and being paid for on the borrowing side through IFM are separate."

"We do order some preprints and pay for them but have not developed a full preprint policy. We decide on a case-by-case basis," Lieberthal adds.

Unmediated or Mediated Access to Document Delivery Services

Almost everything is mediated by the ILL staff, except for Direct Request from WorldCat. The department does not place limits, except that staff will not purchase dissertations for undergraduates. "We find most times they didn't realize it was a dissertation and they don't really want it," Lieberthal notes.

Fee-Based Services

"If we need an item and the library that can provide it charges, we will pay the fee," Lieberthal states. "We only use a commercial document supplier when an item is not easily available via OCLC. We do not have a document delivery service for outside users. All lending requests come through OCLC with an occasional ALA form or FAX request."

Best Management Advice for Other Academic ILL Departments

"When you have to, use a supplier," advises Lieberthal. "Otherwise, if you can easily obtain an item in a timely manner through a cooperating library, do so. That way you have control over copyright fees and you can use the "Rule of Five." When you use a document supplier you pay copyright fees for everything. Some items can only be obtained through document suppliers because of restrictions on making copies in some databases. Some items are only available at one vendor, for example, the journal *Zootaxa* is only available from CISTI."

VI. Copyright and Licensing

ILL Copyright-Compliant Policy or Guidelines

Departmental staff track copyright through their ILLiad software. The department pays CCC once a year. Staff purchase many items through the British Library and pay copyright up front for that material. Staff follow the "Rule of Five." If the copyright report shows fees that need to be paid directly through the publisher, staff do their best to contact them and pay them separately, though this rarely occurs.

Licensing

"When we lend items from our electronic databases, we print the item and then scan it out," Lieberthal says. "We don't send out PDF attachments directly through any databases. This can also be achieved by using DocMorph or MyMorph to convert a PDF into a tiff file to send out via Ariel. The Head of ILL continues to advocate for ILL permissions in any new database."

VII. Institutional Repositories and Open Access

"We will only change our workflow if we can't find the item anywhere else," Lieberthal maintains. "We do not stop our workflow to check for items that are free on the Internet. If an item is in our online journal holdings, we send the request back to the user or into the document delivery queue to deliver the item to the patron. We do this whether the item is in an open source or paid database. Our lending and borrowing request numbers have not noticeably been affected by these open access materials."

VIII. Service Priorities for Constituents

All constituents receive free ILL service. "Our only restrictions are that we don't borrow reserves or textbooks," notes Lieberthal. "This issue comes up with undergraduates and graduates."

ILL Services for Community Members, Visiting Scholars or Other Institutions

The department provides free requests for emeritus professors and offers free service to visiting scholars and Empire State and campus Round Table members. The department also provides five free requests a year for Friends of the Library and members of the alumni association. Service is not provided for community members.

Special Services to Constituents

"We provide free document delivery for faculty and staff of any printed journal article in our collection," Lieberthal reports. "We will scan the item and deliver it electronically through ILLiad to the patron. This service is also available to students at our Southampton and Manhattan campuses. Occasionally we will scan or photograph special items and deliver them electronically or on a CD. Examples include very old and fragile items, which won't copy well."

"If a patron calls we will provide reference assistance," adds Lieberthal. "Reference librarians will also refer people to our expert bibliographic searcher. We have a separate ILL office on the first floor of the library and patrons come in to pick up their items. They know where to find us and that helps to encourage patrons to ask questions. Questions also come in through the ILL generic email address and through our AskLibrarian chat and email service when reference librarians refer questions on to the ILL department."

Notification and Delivery of Materials

Most notification is done automatically through e-mail. The department delivers journal articles and book chapters electronically and will also make print copies of articles for pickup in the ILL office. All books obtained through ILL are picked up by the patron in the ILL office and returned there as well. Pickup is limited to the ILL office and three remote locations, Marine and Atmospheric Sciences (MASIC), Manhattan and Southampton. All patrons from other closer branches (Physics/Math, Chemistry) pick up in the ILL office in the main library.

IX. Services to Distance Learning Students

"Electronic delivery of articles by ILL is a big advantage and this service is offered to all our users, including distance education students," says Lieberthal. "We do not have a large distance learning department at Stony Brook."

"Students in our remote location can request any item for themselves, and we will deliver it to their branch," adds Lieberthal. "They can submit a document delivery request through ILLiad or arrange it through their local circulation department. Our document delivery service is normally restricted to faculty and staff. But for our distance learners — i.e., Manhattan and Southampton, this service is available to students as well. We also provide document delivery to students and faculty doing fieldwork in remote locations."

ILL services are free for all students, including distance education constituents. The reciprocal arrangement with other SUNY universities and colleges also applies to distance education all requests.

X. Special Collections

Most special collections items do not get lent out. "If there are multiple copies, we might send the copy," says Lieberthal. "If not we scan, Xerox or refuse the request. If the request comes through ILL, both departments work on it. If the requests come from individuals or libraries without OCLC ILL capabilities, they contact special collections themselves. We do not have a very large volume of requests for special collections. As it stands now, we handle requests on a case-by-case basis."

XI. Measuring Productivity and Evaluating Services

"We run reports annually and as we need them," Lieberthal reports. "Traditional means of gauging success like turnaround time are not always a good measure of service for a large research university such as ours. Some faculty members or graduate students might request abstruse items and don't care how long it takes us to find them. For example, if someone is looking for the whole run of a newspaper in a foreign country for a particular year or years, it might take a month or two to find a library which has it and will lend out the microfilm. This one request might add a day on to all our other borrowing requests for the month it is tallied, so turnaround time is not a good measure of our productivity."

"The only other means of assessing our productivity has come to us in the form of compliments to the dean of the library about our excellent service, acknowledgments in the books published by our faculty and mention of our service in documents written by faculty to the administration," mentions Lieberthal. "Our primary bibliographic searcher has received both the President's award for excellence in professional service and the excellence award from the Graduate Students' Association."

OTHER REPORTS OF INTEREST FROM PRIMARY RESEARCH GROUP

THE INTERNATIONAL SURVEY OF LIBRARY & MUSEUM DIGITIZATION PROJECTS
ISBN: 1-57440-105-X   Price: $89.50   October 2008

The International Survey of Library & Museum Digitization Projects presents detailed data about the management and development of a broad range of library special collection and museum digitization projects. Data are broken out by type of digitization project (i.e., text, photograph, film, audio, etc.) size and type of institution, annual spending on digitization and other variables. The report presents data and narrative on staffing, training, funding, technology selection, outsourcing, permissions and copyright clearance, cataloging, digital asset management, software and applications selection, marketing and many other issues of interest to libraries and museums that are digitizing aspects of their collections.

THE SURVEY OF ACADEMIC & RESEARCH LIBRARY JOURNAL PURCHASING PRACTICES
ISBN: 1-57440-108-4   Price: $89.50   November 2008

This report looks closely at the acquisition practices for scientific, technical and academic journals of academic and research libraries. Some of the many issues covered: attitudes toward the pricing and digital access policies of select major journals publishers, preferences for print, print/electronic access combinations, and electronic access alone arrangements. Covers spending plans, preferences for use of consortiums, and use of, and evaluation of subscription agents. Charts attitudes toward CLOCKSS, open access, use of URL resolvers and other pressing issues of interest to major purchasers of academic and technical journals.

ACADEMIC LIBRARY CATALOGING PRACTICES BENCHMARKS
ISBN: 1-57440-106-8   Price: $89.50   November 2008

This 254-page report presents data from a survey of the cataloging practices of approximately 80 North American academic libraries. In more than 630 tables of data and related commentary from participating librarians and our analysts, the report gives a broad overview of academic library cataloging practices related to outsourcing, selection and deployment of personnel, salaries, the state of continuing education in cataloging, and much more. Data are broken out by size and type of college and for public and private colleges. Survey participants also discuss how they define the cataloger's range of responsibilities, how they train their catalogers, how they assess cataloging quality, whether they use cataloging quotas or other measures to spur productivity, what software and other cataloging technology they use and why, how they make outsourcing decisions and more.

SURVEY OF ACADEMIC LIBRARY USE OF INSTRUCTIONAL TECHNOLOGY:
ISBN: 1-57440-107-6   Price: $85.00   October 2008

The Survey of Academic Library Use of Instructional Technology examines use of information literacy computer labs, classroom response "clicker" technology, whiteboards, and many other educational technologies used by libraries. In an era in which library education has become an increasingly important part of the academic librarian's duties, this report provides insights on how peer institutions are allocating their educational budgets and choosing the most effective technologies and practices in information and general library literacy.

CORPORATE LIBRARY BENCHMARKS, 2009 Edition
ISBN 1-57440-109-2   Publication Date: December 2008 Price: $195.00

Corporate Library Benchmarks, 2009 Edition presents extensive data from 52 corporate and other business-oriented libraries; data is broken out by company size, type of industry and other criteria.

The mean number of employees for the organizations in the sample is 16,000; the median, 1700. Some of the many issues covered in the report are: spending on electronic and print forms of books, directories, journals and other information resources; library staffing trends, number of library locations maintained and the allocation of office space to the library, disputes with publishers, allocation of library staff time, level of awareness of database contract terms of peer institutions, reference workload, and the overall level of influence of the library in corporate decision making.

LIBRARY USE OF E-BOOKS
ISBN: 1-57440-101-7 Price: $75.00   Publication Date: April 2008

Data in the report are based on a survey of 75 academic, public and special libraries. Data are broken out by library budget size, for U.S. and non-U.S. libraries and for academic and non-academic libraries. The report presents more than 300 tables of data on e-book use by libraries, as well as analysis and commentary. Librarians detail their plans on how they plan to develop their e-book collections, what they think of e-book readers and software, and which e-book aggregators and publishers appeal to them most and why. Other issues covered include: library production of e-books and collection digitization, e-book collection information literacy efforts, use of e-books in course reserves and inter-library loan, e-book pricing and inflation issues, acquisition sources and strategies for e-books and other issues of concern to libraries and book publishers.

LAW LIBRARY BENCHMARKS, 2008-09 EDITION
ISBN: 1-57440-104-1   Price: $129.00   Publication Date: October 2008

Data in the report are based on a survey of 55 North American law libraries drawn from law firm, private company, university, courthouse and government agency law libraries. Data are broken out by size and type of library for ease in benchmarking. The 120+ page report covers developments in staffing, salaries, budgets, materials spending, use of blogs & wikis, use of legal directories, the library role in knowledge management, records management and content management systems. Patron and librarian training, reimbursement for library-related education and other issues are also covered in this latest edition.

RESEARCH LIBRARY INTERNATIONAL BENCHMARKS
ISBN: 1-57440-103-3   Publication Date: June 2008   Price: $95.00

Research Library International Benchmarks presents data from a survey of 45 major research libraries from the U.S., Australia, Canada, Spain, the U.K., Japan and others. Data are presented separately for university, government/non-profit and corporate/legal libraries, and for U.S. and non-U.S. libraries, as well as by size of library and type of library, corporate/legal, university and government. The 200-page report presents a broad range of data on current and planned materials, salary, info technology and capital spending, hiring plans, spending trends for e-books, journals, books and much, much more. Provides data on trends in discount margins from vendors, relations with consortiums, information literacy efforts, workstation, laptop and learning space development, use of scanners and digital cameras, use of RFID technology, federated search and many other pressing issues for major research libraries, university and otherwise.

THE SURVEY OF LIBRARY DATABASE LICENSING PRACTICES
ISBN: 1-57440-093-2   Price: $80.00   Publication Date: December 2007

The study presents data from 90 libraries – corporate, legal, college, public, state and nonprofit libraries – about their database licensing practices. More than half of the participating libraries are from the U.S., and the rest are from Canada, Australia, the U.K. and other countries. Data are broken out by library type and size of library, as well as for overall level of database expenditure. The 100+-page study, with more than 400 tables and charts, presents benchmarking data enabling librarians to compare their library's practices to peers in many areas related to licensing. Metrics provided include: percentage of licenses from consortiums, spending on consortium dues, time spent seeking new consortium partners, number of consortium memberships maintained; growth rate in the percentage of licenses obtained through consortiums; expectation for consortium purchases in the future; number of licenses, growth rate in the number of licenses, spending on licenses for directories, electronic journals, e-books and magazine/newspaper databases; future spending plans on all of the above; price inflation experienced for electronic resources in business, medical, humanities, financial, market research, social sciences and many other information categories; price inflation for e-books, electronic directories, journals and newspaper/magazine databases; percentage of licenses that require passwords; percentage of licenses that have simultaneous access restrictions; spending on legal services related to licenses; and much more.

THE INTERNATIONAL SURVEY OF INSTITUTIONAL DIGITAL REPOSITORIES
ISBN: 1-57440-090-8   Price: $89.50   Publication Date: November 2007

The study presents data from 56 institutional digital repositories from 11 countries, including the U.S., Canada, Australia, Germany, South Africa, India, Turkey and other countries. The 121-page study presents more than 300 tables of data and commentary and is based on data from higher education libraries and other institutions involved in institutional digital repository development. In more than 300 tables and associated commentary, the report describes norms and benchmarks for budgets, software use, manpower needs and deployment, financing, usage, marketing and other facets of the management of international digital repositories. The report helps to answer questions such as: who contributes to the repositories and on what terms? Who uses the repositories? What do they contain and how fast are they growing in terms of content and end use? What measures have repositories used to gain faculty and other researcher participation? How successful have these methods been? How has the repository been marketed and cataloged? What has been the financial impact? Data are broken out by size and type of institution for easier benchmarking.

PREVAILING & BEST PRACTICES IN ELECTRONIC AND PRINT SERIALS MANAGEMENT
ISBN: 1-57440-076-2   Price: $80.00   Publication Date: November 2005

This report looks closely at the electronic and print serials procurement and management practices of 11 libraries, including: the University of Ohio, Villanova University, the Colorado School of Mines, Carleton College, Northwestern University, Baylor University, Princeton University, the University of Pennsylvania, the University of San Francisco, Embry-Riddle Aeronautical University and the University of Nebraska Medical Center. The report looks at both electronic and print serials and includes discussions of the following issues: selection and management of serials agents, including the negotiation of payment; allocating the serials budget by department; resolving access issues with publishers; use of consortiums in journal licensing; invoice reconciliation and payment; periodicals binding, claims, check-in and management; serials department staff size and range of responsibilities; serials management software; use of open access archives and university depositories; policies on gift subscriptions, free trials and academic exchanges of publications; use of electronic serials/catalog linking technology; acquisition of usage statistics; cooperative arrangements with other local libraries and other issues in serials management.

CORPORATE LIBRARY BENCHMARKS, 2007 Edition
ISBN: 1-57440-084-3   Price: $189.00

This report, our sixth survey of corporate libraries, presents a broad range of data, broken out by size and type of organization. Among the issues covered are: spending trends on books, magazines, journals, databases, CD-ROMs, directories and other information vehicles, plans to augment or reduce the scope and size of the corporate library, hiring plans, salary spending and personnel use, librarian research priorities by type of subject matter, policies on information literacy and library education, library relations with management, budget trends, breakdown in spending by the library versus other corporate departments that procure information, librarian use of blogs and RSS feeds, level of discounts received from book jobbers, use of subscription agents, and other issues of concern to corporate and other business librarians.

EMERGING ISSUES IN ACADEMIC LIBRARY CATALOGING & TECHNICAL SERVICES
ISBN: 1-57440-086-X   Price: $72.50   Publication Date: April 2007

This report presents nine highly detailed case studies of leading university cataloging and technical service departments. It provides insights into how they are handling 10 major changes facing them, including: the encouragement of cataloging productivity; impact of new technologies on and enhancement of online catalogs; the transition to metadata standards; the cataloging of Websites and digital and other special collections; library catalog and metadata training; database maintenance, holdings and physical processing; managing the relationship with acquisitions departments; staff education; and other important issues. Survey participants represent academic libraries of varying sizes and classifications, with many different viewpoints. Universities surveyed are: Brigham Young; Curry College; Haverford College; Illinois, Louisiana and Pennsylvania State Universities; University of North Dakota; University of Washington; and Yale University.

THE MARKETING OF HISTORIC SITES, MUSEUMS, EXHIBITS AND ARCHIVES
ISBN: 1-57440-074-6   Price: $95.00   Publication Date: June 2005

This report looks closely at how history is presented and marketed by organizations such as history museums, libraries, historical societies, and historic sites and monuments. The report profiles the efforts of the Vermont Historical Society, Hook's Historic Drug Store and Pharmacy, the Thomas Jefferson Foundation/Monticello, the Musee Conti Wax Museum of New Orleans, the Bostonian Society, the Dittrick Medical History Center, the Band Museum, the Belmont Mansion, the Kansas State Historical Society, the Computer History Museum, the Atari Virtual Museum, the Museum of American Financial History, the Atlanta History Center and the public libraries of Denver and Evansville. The study's revealing profiles, based on extensive interviews with executive directors and marketing managers of the institutions cited, provide a deeply detailed look at how history museums, sites, societies and monuments are marketing themselves.

LICENSING AND COPYRIGHT MANAGEMENT: BEST PRACTICES OF COLLEGE, SPECIAL AND RESEARCH LIBRARIES
ISBN: 1-57440-068-1   Price: $80 Publication Date: May 2004

This report looks closely at the licensing and copyright-management strategies of a sample of leading research, college and special libraries and consortiums and includes interviews with leading experts. The focus is on electronic-database licensing, and includes discussions of the most pressing issues: development of consortiums and group buying initiatives, terms of access, liability for infringement, archiving, training and development, free-trial periods, contract language, contract-management software and time-management issues, acquiring and using usage statistics, elimination of duplication, enhancement of bargaining power, open-access publishing policies, interruption-of-service contingency arrangements, changes in pricing over the life of the contract, interlibrary loan of electronic files, copyright clearance, negotiating tactics, uses of consortiums, and many other issues. The report profiles the emergence of consortiums and group-buying arrangements.

TRENDS IN TRAINING COLLEGE FACULTY, STUDENTS & STAFF IN COMPUTER LITERACY
ISBN: 1-57440-085-1   Price: $67.50   Publication Date: April 2007

This report looks closely at how nine institutions of higher education are approaching the question of training faculty, staff and students in the use of educationally oriented information technologies. The report helps answer questions such as: what is the most productive way to help faculty master new information technologies? How much should be spent on such training? What are the best practices? How should distance learning instructors be trained? How formal, and how ad-hoc, should training efforts be? What should computer literacy standards be among students? How can subject-specific computer literacy be integrated into curriculums? Should colleges develop their own training methods, buy packaged solutions, find them on the Web?

Organizations profiled are: Brooklyn Law School, Florida State University College of Medicine, Indiana University Southeast, Texas Christian University, Clemson University, the Teaching & Learning Technology Group, the Appalachian College Association, Tuskegee Institute and the University of West Georgia.

THE SURVEY OF LIBRARY CAFÉS
ISBN: 1-57440-089-4   Price: $75.00   Publication Date: 2007

The Survey of Library Cafés presents data from more than 40 academic and public libraries about their cafés and other foodservice operations. The 60-page report gives extensive data and commentary on library café sales volume, best-selling products, impacts on library maintenance costs, reasons for starting a café, effects on library traffic, and many other issues regarding the decision to start and manage a library café.